BIRDS
of
SAN DIEGO

Chris C. Fisher
Herbert Clarke

LONE
PINE

The Publisher: Lone Pine Publishing

1901 Raymond Ave. SW, Suite C	206, 10426 – 81 Ave.	202A, 1110 Seymour St.
Renton, WA 98055	Edmonton, AB T6E 1X5	Vancouver, BC V6B 3N3
USA	Canada	Canada

Canadian Cataloguing in Publication Data

Fisher, Chris C. (Christopher Charles)
    Birds of San Diego

Includes bibliographical references and index.
ISBN 1-55105-102-8

    1. Birds—California—San Diego—Identification. 2. Bird watching—California—San Diego. I. Clarke, Herbert, 1927– II. Nordhagen, Ted. III. Ross, Gary, 1961– IV. Title.
QL684.C2F565 1997   598'.09794'985   C97-910645-1

Senior Editor: Nancy Foulds
Project Editor: Roland Lines
Technical Review: Wayne Campbell
Production Manager: David Dodge
Production and Layout: Michelle Bynoe
Book Design: Carol S. Dragich
Cover Design: Jun Lee
Cover Illustration: Gary Ross
Map: Volker Bodegom
Illustrations: Gary Ross, Ted Nordhagen, Ewa Pluciennik, Horst Krause
Separations and Film: Elite Lithographers Co. Ltd., Edmonton, Alberta, Canada
Printing: Quality Colour Press Inc., Edmonton, Alberta, Canada

The publisher gratefully acknowledges the assistance of the Department of Canadian Heritage and Alberta Community Development, and the financial support provided by the Alberta Foundation for the Arts.

Contents

Acknowledgments

A book such as this is made possible by the inspired work of San Diego's naturalist community, whose contributions continue to advance the science of ornithology and to motivate a new generation of nature lovers.

My thanks go to Gary Ross and Ted Nordhagen, whose illustrations have elevated the quality of this book; to Carole Patterson, for her continual support; to the birding societies of the San Diego area, which all make daily contributions to natural history; to the team at Lone Pine Publishing—Roland Lines, Nancy Foulds, Eloise Pulos, Greg Brown, Michelle Bynoe and Shane Kennedy—for their input and steering; to John Acorn and Jim Butler, for their stewardship and their remarkable passion; and, finally, to Herbert Clarke and Wayne Campbell, premier naturalists whose works have served as models of excellence, for their thorough and helpful review of the text.

Chris C. Fisher

Introduction

No matter where we live, birds are a natural part of our lives. We are so used to seeing them that we often take their presence for granted. When we take the time to notice their colors, songs and behaviors, we experience their dynamic appeal.

This book presents a brief introduction into the lives of birds. It is intended to serve as both a bird identification guide and a bird appreciation guide. Getting to know the names of birds is the first step toward getting to know birds. Once we've made contact with a species, we can better appreciate its character and mannerisms during future encounters. Over a lifetime of meetings, many birds become acquaintances, some seen daily, others not for years.

The selection of species within this book represents a balance between the familiar and the noteworthy. Many of the 125 species described in this guide are the most common species found in the San Diego area. Some are less common, but they are noteworthy because they are important ecologically or because their particular status grants them a high profile. It would be impossible for a beginners' book such as this to comprehensively describe all the birds found in the San Diego area. Furthermore, there is no one site where all the species within this book can be observed simultaneously, but most species can be viewed—at least seasonally—within a short drive (or sail) from San Diego. The San Diego area is blessed with excellent bird-finding guides (Childs 1993, Holt 1990 and Unitt 1984) that will help birders looking for a specific species.

It is hoped that this guide will inspire novice birdwatchers into spending some time outdoors, gaining valuable experience with the local bird community. This book stresses the identity of birds, but it also attempts to bring them to life by discussing their various character traits. We often discuss a bird's character traits in human terms, because personifying a bird's character can help us to feel a bond with the birds. The perceived links with birds should not be mistaken for actual behaviors, as our interpretations may falsely reflect the complexities of bird life.

FEATURES OF THE LANDSCAPE

From ocean to mountains, grasslands to marshes and deserts to wood-lands, the natural environment around San Diego offers more distinct and unique types of habitats for birds than almost any other city in the country, which in turn provides many opportune spots for observing bird life at any time of the year. Best of all, most of these birding areas can be reached within a single day's travel.

The greatest diversity of birds occurs over the winter months, when mi-grants from the north and from the interior retreat to San Diego for the coast's warm, moist weather. Spring is also a busy time of year: migrating songbirds drift through our area on their way to the low-elevation passes in the coastal mountains that they use to reach their northern breeding grounds. In fall, the southeastern slant of the southern California coast-line combines with the southward movements of migrating birds to cre-ate 'migrant traps.' Many birds congregate in areas where they run into the open ocean. The Tijuana River Valley is one of the best places in the country to see rare migrants, out-of-range vagrants and local specialties.

San Diego's unique collection of lagoons, bays, freshwater marshes and estuaries supports an interesting and assorted array of bird life. During the winter months, sandpipers and plovers are commonly seen foraging in San Diego's tidal mudflats and estuaries. A refuge for many gulls, her-ons, ducks and shorebirds, the San Diego Bay and Mission Bay areas are always interesting places to visit. Although few species inhabit the city's sandy beaches, the kelp that is washed up here provides good foraging habitat for many shorebirds.

Our more rugged coastlines are home to Brown Pelicans, cormorants and other coastal birds, especially during winter. The rocky shores at La Jolla and Torrey Pines are good locations to find coastal birds. Small, rocky islands offshore provide a summer retreat for many seabirds, cormorants and gulls to build their nests and raise their young.

The distribution of California's seabirds is greatly influenced by the ocean currents off San Diego's shores. During late autumn, San Diego has some of the most intriguing pelagic and coastal birdlife in the country. Tropical seabirds, such as the Magnificent Frigatebird and the Red-billed Tropicbird, are often spotted offshore. The upwelling of cold, nutrient-rich waters off the San Diego coast may also explain the appearance of such species as the Black-footed Albatross, the Sooty Shearwater and the Black Storm-Petrel.

San Diego's broadleaf forests, including small pockets in backyards and city parks, are where you will find most of our songbirds. Busy with the

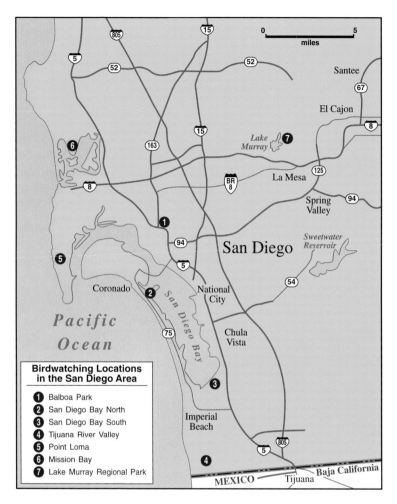

Birdwatching Locations
in the San Diego Area

1 Balboa Park
2 San Diego Bay North
3 San Diego Bay South
4 Tijuana River Valley
5 Point Loma
6 Mission Bay
7 Lake Murray Regional Park

activity of migrating birds in spring, oak and sycamore forests come alive
with the incessant chattering of sparrows and warblers. These forests are
also permanent homes to such species as the Western Screech-Owl, the
Cooper's Hawk and the Western Bluebird. Not all our songbirds are migrants, and there are many species that can tolerate our hot, dry summers:
Bullock's Orioles and Hutton's Vireos raise their broods in the native
black oak and sycamore groves; Wrentits, California Thrashers and Western Kingbirds nest in the coastal scrub and chaparral brushland.

Although you might not expect it, desert communities also harbor a great
concentration of migrating birds. During spring, natural oases and water
sources become inland 'migrant traps,' providing food, water and shelter
for many tired and thirsty travelers.

THE IMPORTANCE OF HABITAT

Understanding the relationship between habitat and bird species often helps identify which birds are which. Because you won't find a loon up a tree or a quail out at sea, habitat is an important thing to note when birdwatching.

The quality of habitat is one of the most powerful factors to influence bird distribution, and with experience you may become amazed by the predictability of some birds within a specific habitat type. The habitat icons in this book show where each species can most commonly be found. It is important to realize, however, that because of their migratory habits, birds are sometimes found in completely different habitats.

Habitat Icons
Each bird in this guide is accompanied by at least one habitat symbol, which represents a general environment where the bird is most likely to be seen. Most birds will be seen within their associated habitat, but migrants can turn up in just about any habitat type. These unexpected surprises (despite being confusing to novice birders) are among the most powerful motivations for the increasing legion of birdwatchers.

Ocean
and Bays

Coastal
Shoreline

Estuaries
and Marshes

Grasslands
and Fields

Chaparral
and Brushland

Broadleaf
Forests

Parks and
Gardens

Coniferous
Forests

THE ORGANIZATION OF THIS BOOK

To simplify field identification, *Birds of San Diego* is organized slightly differently from many other field guides that use strict phylogenetic groupings. In cases where many birds from the same family are described, conventional groupings are maintained. In other cases, however, distantly related birds that share physical and behavioral similarities are grouped together. This blend of family grouping and physically similar super-groups strives to help the novice birdwatcher identify and appreciate the birds he or she encounters.

DIVING BIRDS

loons, grebes, pelicans, cormorants

These heavy-bodied birds are adapted to diving for their food. Between their underwater foraging dives, they are most frequently seen on the surface of the water. These birds could only be confused with one another or with certain diving ducks.

OCEAN BIRDS

shearwaters

These long-winged birds of the open ocean come ashore on remote islands and shores only to breed. They are excellent fliers, giving only a few deep wing beats between long glides. They are typically seen skimming low over the water, well off shore.

WETLAND WADERS

herons, egrets, soras, coots
Although this group varies considerably in size, and represents two separate families of birds, wetland waders share similar habitat and food preferences. Some of these long-legged birds of marshes are quite common, but certain species are heard far more than they are seen.

WATERFOWL

geese, ducks
Waterfowl tend to have stout bodies and webbed feet, and they are swift in flight. Although most species are associated with water, waterfowl can sometimes be seen grazing on upland sites.

VULTURES, HAWKS AND FALCONS

vultures, kites, hawks, kestrels
From deep forests to open country to large lakes, there are hawks, kites and falcons hunting the skies. Their predatory look—with sharp talons, hooked bills and forward-facing eyes—easily identifies this group. Hawks generally forage during the day, and many use their broad wings to soar in thermals and updrafts.

QUAILS

These gamebirds bear a superficial resemblance to chickens. They are stout birds and poor flyers, and they are most often encountered on the ground or when flushed.

SHOREBIRDS

plovers, avocets, godwits, sandpipers, etc.

Shorebirds are usually confined to the shores and tidal flats of the ocean and bays. Although these small, long-legged, swift-flying birds are mainly found in our estuaries, don't be surprised to find certain species in pastures and marshy areas.

GULLS AND TERNS

gulls, terns, skimmers

Gulls are relatively large, usually light-colored birds that are frequently seen swimming in salt- or freshwater, walking about in urban areas or soaring gracefully over the city. Their backs tend to be darker than their bellies, and their feet are webbed. Terns are in the same family as gulls, but they are not often seen on the ground, they rarely soar and they have straight, pointed bills.

DOVES

All our doves are easily recognizable. Rock Doves are found in all urban areas, from city parks to the downtown core. These urban doves have many of the same physical and behavioral characteristics as the 'wilder' Band-tailed Pigeons and Mourning Doves.

NOCTURNAL BIRDS

owls, nighthawks

These night hunters all have large eyes. The owls, which primarily prey on rodents, have powerful, taloned feet and strongly hooked bills. Nighthawks catch moths and other nocturnal insects on the wing. Although owls are primarily active at night, their distinctive calls enable birdwatchers to readily identify them.

WOODPECKERS

The drumming sound of hammering wood and their precarious foraging habits easily identify most woodpeckers. They are frequently seen in forests, clinging to trunks and chipping away bark with their straight, sturdy bills. Even when these birds cannot be seen or heard, the characteristic marks of certain species can be seen on trees in any mature forest.

HUMMINGBIRDS

Hummingbirds are this area's smallest birds. Their bright colors and swift flight are very characteristic.

FLYCATCHERS

flycatchers, phoebes, kingbirds
This family is perhaps best identified by its foraging behavior. As the name implies, flycatchers catch insects on the wing, darting after them from a favorite perch. Most flycatchers sing simple but distinctive songs. Many flycatchers have subdued plumage, but phoebes and kingbirds are rather colorful.

SWIFTS AND SWALLOWS

Members of these two families are typically seen at their nest sites or in flight. Small but sleek, swifts and swallows have narrow wings and short tails, and they are nearly always seen in flight. Although swallows are superficially similar to swifts in behavior and appearance, the two groups are not closely related.

JAYS AND CROWS

scrub-jays, crows, ravens
Many members of this family can be identified by their intelligence and adaptability. They are easily observed birds that are frequently extremely bold, teasing the animal-human barrier. They are sometimes called 'corvids,' from Corvidae, the scientific name for the family.

SMALL SONGBIRDS

titmice, nuthatches, wrens, kinglets, etc.

Birds in this group are all generally smaller than a sparrow. Many of them associate with one another in mixed-species flocks. With the exception of the Marsh Wren, most are commonly encountered in city parks, backyards and other wooded areas.

BLUEBIRDS AND THRUSHES

bluebirds, thrushes, robins

From the robin to the secretive forest thrushes, this group of beautiful singers has the finest collective voice. Although some thrushes are very familiar, others require a little experience and patience to identify.

VIREOS AND WARBLERS

Warblers are splashed liberally with colors, while vireos tend to dress in pale olive. These birds are all very small woodland birds that sing characteristic courtship songs.

MID-SIZED SONGBIRDS

tanagers, mockingbirds, waxwings, starlings, etc.

The birds within this group are all sized between a sparrow and a robin. Tanagers are very colorful and sing complex, flute-like songs, while the tan-colored waxwings are more reserved in dress and voice. Starlings and mockingbirds are frequently seen and heard all over our area.

SPARROWS

towhees, sparrows, juncos

These small, often indistinct birds are predominantly brown. Their songs are often very useful in identification. Many birdwatchers discount many of these sparrows as simply 'little brown birds'; this is unfortunate, since these birds are worthy of the extra identification effort. The Spotted Towhee is a colorful exception in the sparrow subfamily.

BLACKBIRDS AND ORIOLES

blackbirds, meadowlarks, cowbirds, orioles

Most of these birds are predominantly black and have relatively long tails. They are common in open areas, city parks and agricultural fields. Western Meadowlarks belong in the blackbird family despite not being black and having short tails.

FINCH-LIKE BIRDS

finches, grosbeaks, buntings, house sparrow

These finches and finch-like birds are primarily adapted to feeding on seeds, and they have stout, conical bills. Many are birdfeeder regulars, and they are a familiar part of the winter scene. Grosbeaks and buntings are very colorful and sing complex, flute-like songs.

ABUNDANCE CHARTS

Jan Feb Mar Apr May Jun Jul Aug Sept Oct Nov Dec

Accompanying each bird description is a chart that indicates the relative abundance of the species throughout the year. These stylized graphs offer some insight into the distribution and abundance of the birds, but they should not be viewed as definitive; they represent a generalized overview. There may be inconsistencies specific to time and location, but these charts should provide readers with a basic reference for bird abundance and occurrence.

Each chart is divided into the 12 months of the year. The pale orange that colors the chart is an indication of abundance: the more color, the more common the bird. Dark orange is used to indicate the nesting period. The time frame of breeding is approximate, and nesting birds can certainly be found both before and after the period indicated on the chart. Where no nesting color is shown, the bird breeds outside the area—mainly to the north and east—and visits San Diego in significant numbers during migration or in winter.

These graphs are based on personal observations and on *A Birder's Guide to Southern California* (Holt 1990).

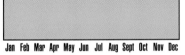

Jan Feb Mar Apr May Jun Jul Aug Sept Oct Nov Dec
abundant

Jan Feb Mar Apr May Jun Jul Aug Sept Oct Nov Dec
common

Jan Feb Mar Apr May Jun Jul Aug Sept Oct Nov Dec
uncommon

Jan Feb Mar Apr May Jun Jul Aug Sept Oct Nov Dec
rare

Jan Feb Mar Apr May Jun Jul Aug Sept Oct Nov Dec
unlikely

Jan Feb Mar Apr May Jun Jul Aug Sept Oct Nov Dec
absent

BIRDS
of SAN DIEGO

Pacific Loon
Gavia pacifica

Although wintering Pacific Loons do not sport their summer velvet suit, what they lack in style they more than compensate for in numbers. All along the California coast, Pacific Loons are among the most common of loons, swaying gingerly on the ever-moving surf. Flocks can be easily observed from shoreline viewpoints, such as Cabrillo National Monument, during the winter months.

Like many wintering seabirds, Pacific Loons hunt small fish. These loons routinely poke their heads underwater, looking for potential prey and plotting pursuit. They dive deeply and efficiently, compressing their feathers to reduce underwater drag and to decrease their buoyancy. Propelling themselves primarily with their rear-set legs, these birds can outswim many fish over short distances. They are often observed bringing their catch up to the surface, where it is tossed down their throat head first with a quick upward nod of the bill.

Similar Species: Common Loon has a heavier bill and its nape is darker than its back. Red-throated Loon has extensive white spots on its back. Cormorants (pp. 23–24) have longer necks.

non-breeding

Quick I.D.: goose-sized; slender, straight bill; sexes similar. *Non-breeding:* black cap extends through eyes; dark upperparts; light underparts; nape lighter than back; steep forehead.
Size: 23–29 in.

Jan Feb Mar Apr May Jun Jul Aug Sept Oct Nov Dec

Pied-billed Grebe

Podilymbus podiceps

breeding

The small, stout, drab body of the Pied-billed Grebe seems perfectly suited to its marshy habitat, but the loud, whooping *kuk-kuk-cow-cow-cow-cowp-cowp* it makes is a sound that seems more at home in tropical rainforests.

Pied-billed Grebes can be found on most freshwater wetlands that are surrounded by cattails, bulrushes or other emergent vegetation. These diving birds are frustrating to follow as they disappear and then reappear among the water-lilies of urban wetlands.

Many Pied-billed Grebes remain in the area during summer, often nesting within view of lakeside trails. They build nests that float on the water's surface, and their eggs often rest in waterlogged vegetation. Young grebes take their first swim soon after hatching, but they will instinctively clamber aboard a parent's back at the first sign of danger.

Similar Species: Eared Grebe (p. 20) and Horned Grebe have light underparts. Ducks (pp. 34–43) have bills that are flattened top to bottom.

Jan Feb Mar Apr May Jun Jul Aug Sept Oct Nov Dec

Quick I.D.: smaller than a duck; all-brown; sexes similar. *Breeding:* dark vertical band on thick, pale bill; black chin. *First-year young* (summer/fall): striped brown and white.
Size: 12–14 in.

Eared Grebe

Podiceps nigricollis

non-breeding

Like many waterbirds that winter in the San Diego area, Eared Grebes lose their splendid summer plumage and assume a low-key, gray-and-white coloring. So dramatic is their transformation that from their summer wardrobe (seen briefly in April before their departure) only their blood-red eyes remain.

Eared Grebes are common in protected bays and along ocean coasts from September through April. They are commonly seen on lagoons and bays. Their behavior is characteristically peppy: they leap up before neatly diving headfirst into the water.

All grebes eat feathers, a seemingly strange habit that frequently causes their digestive systems to become packed. It is thought that this behavior may protect their stomachs from sharp fish bones, and it may also slow the passage of food through the digestive system so that more nutrients can be absorbed.

Similar Species: Horned Grebe has a white cheek and a heavier bill. Western Grebe (p. 21) is much larger and has a long bill, a long neck and a white cheek.

Quick I.D.: smaller than a duck; thin bill; sexes similar.
Non-breeding: dark cheek and upperparts; light underparts; white ear patch.
Size: 12–14 in.

Jan Feb Mar Apr May Jun Jul Aug Sept Oct Nov Dec

Western Grebe
Aechmophorus occidentalis

Coastal residents are fortunate to have unsurpassed concentrations of wintering Western Grebes. If you gaze offshore or scan the water at any coastal lagoon or bay, you will frequently have brief, intermittent glimpses of these grebes riding the troughs and peaks of the waves.

The distinguished look of the Western Grebe is refined by its formal plumage, ruby eyes, cobra-like head and long bill. Unlike other over-wintering grebes, the Western Grebe doesn't change its plumage over the seasons. The Western Grebe is easily identified by its long, graceful neck as it fishes the open waters for small fish, which it can occasionally pierce with its dagger-like bill. Grebes have unusual toes: unlike the fully webbed feet of ducks, gulls, cormorants and alcids, grebes' toes are individually lobed.

Similar Species: Clark's Grebe lacks the black through the eyes.

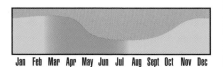

Jan Feb Mar Apr May Jun Jul Aug Sept Oct Nov Dec

Quick I.D.: duck-sized; very long neck; black upperparts; yellow-green bill; black mask through eyes; white underparts; long bill; sexes similar.
Size: 23–28 in.

Brown Pelican
Pelecanus occidentalis

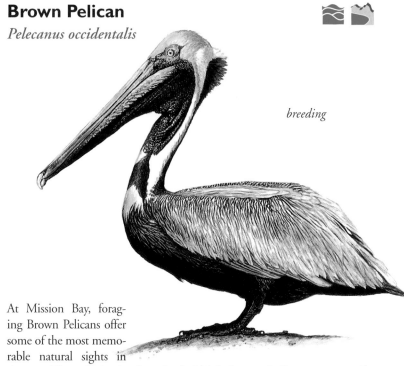

breeding

At Mission Bay, foraging Brown Pelicans offer some of the most memorable natural sights in the area. These distinctive, large-bodied birds frequently forage communally. Unlike the American White Pelican, the Brown Pelican does not forage at the surface of the water. Instead, it is an air-borne hunter. After a flock spots a school of fish, the pelicans wheel about and plunge headfirst in tandem. They open their bills underwater, extending their pouches around the fish. After disappearing beneath the surface for a few instants, the pelicans then jolt back up to the water's surface like corks.

Some people may find that the long, disproportionate bill, deep pouch, great wingspan and dumpy body give this bird a comical look. Whatever your reaction to their appearance, whenever these once-rare birds are encountered, they are sure to instill a sense of awe and admiration.

Similar Species: American White Pelican (uncommon around salt ponds) is all white, and it has black primaries and a dark orange bill.

Quick I.D.: very large; grayish-brown body; gray bill; yellow head; dark belly; sexes similar.
Size: 45–51 in.

Jan Feb Mar Apr May Jun Jul Aug Sept Oct Nov Dec

Double-crested Cormorant
Phalacrocorax auritus

The Double-crested Cormorant is a common sight on the West Coast. Like Pelagic and Brandt's cormorants, Double-crests fly in single-file, low over coastal waters. Only Double-crests, however, are found on inland lakes.

Cormorants lack the ability to waterproof their wings, so they need to dry their wings after each swim. These large, black waterbirds are frequently seen perched on seawalls, bridge pilings and buoys, with their wings partially spread to expose their wet feathers to the sun and the wind. It would seem to be a great disadvantage for a waterbird to have to dry its wings, but the cormorant's ability to wet its feathers decreases its buoyancy, making it easier for it to swim after the fish on which it preys. Sealed nostrils, a long, rudder-like tail and excellent underwater vision are other features of the Double-crested Cormorant's aquatic lifestyle.

breeding

Similar Species: Brandt's Cormorant (p. 24) is slightly larger, flies with its neck outstretched and has a relatively short tail. Pelagic Cormorant is smaller, flies with a straight neck, is iridescent dark green in bright light, and it has white saddle patches and a red throat pouch in breeding plumage. Non-breeding loons (p. 18) and large, dark ducks and geese (pp. 32–43) generally have shorter necks and are more stout overall.

Quick I.D.: goose-sized; all-black; long tail; long neck; sexes similar. *In flight:* kinked neck; rapid wing beats. *Breeding:* bright orange throat pouch; black or white plumes streaming back from eyebrows (seen only at close range). *First-year:* brown; pale neck, breast and belly.
Size: 30–35 in.

Jan Feb Mar Apr May Jun Jul Aug Sept Oct Nov Dec

Brandt's Cormorant

Phalacrocorax penicillatus

The irregular, long lines of flocks of low-flying Brandt's Cormorants are frequently seen off-shore. These common birds do not maintain the tight flocks of other species; instead, their loose lines mirror the peaks and troughs of the waters over which they fly. They are most frequently encountered within a few miles of the seashore; they tend not to travel over great expanses of open water, except in migration.

Brandt's Cormorants are the most abundant cormorant in California. They nest in colonies atop flat rocks on cliffs, at close but well-maintained distances from one another. A few have nested on Point Loma. They are not normally found on inland waters: only rich salmon runs will periodically persuade these marine birds to feast in freshwater.

breeding

Similar Species: Double-crested Cormorant (p. 23) has a proportionally larger head and a pale bill. Pelagic Cormorant is smaller, with a proportionally smaller head and a thinner neck and bill, and it sports white saddle patches in the breeding season.

Quick I.D.: goose-sized; dark overall; light chin strap; long tail; sexes similar. *In flight:* out-stretched neck. *Breeding:* blue throat pouch; fine white plumes on neck and back. *First-year:* dark brown upperparts; pale underparts.
Size: 28–33 in.

Jan Feb Mar Apr May Jun Jul Aug Sept Oct Nov Dec

Sooty Shearwater
Puffinus griseus

Sliding effortlessly on the sea winds, Sooty Shearwaters graze over the tops of waves off our coast. When you are cruising out to Catalina, or other Channel Islands, Sooty Shearwaters will first appear on the horizon as specks that dance effortlessly on outstretched wings over the sea. Should the winds take them past your vessel, these birds of the open marine waters will wing by in a humbling show of their flight skills.

Sooty Shearwaters that grace our coastlines breed on islands off northwestern Mexico. Their post-breeding wanderings take them north in search of animal matter upon which to dine. Although they never touch California soil, these birds can frequently be observed from viewpoints, such as Point Loma, when thousands of shearwaters congregate on anchovy runs around the continental shelf. The concentration of fish draws in shearwaters from hundreds of miles around to feast on the bounty.

Similar Species: Black-vented Shearwater is lighter overall. Immature Heermann's Gull (p. 69) has a black tail and flaps far more frequently. Northern Fulmar lacks the white wing lining and has a thick yellow bill.

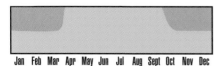

Jan Feb Mar Apr May Jun Jul Aug Sept Oct Nov Dec

Quick I.D.: smaller than a gull; sexes similar. *In flight:* all-dark body; dark bill and feet; faint, white wing lining; wings held in a shallow arch.
Size: 16–18 in.

Great Blue Heron
Ardea herodias

breeding

The Great Blue Heron is one of the largest and most regal of the coastal birds. It often stands motionless as it surveys the calm waters, its graceful lines blending naturally with the grasses and cattails of wetlands. All herons have specialized vertebrae that enable the neck to fold back over itself. The S-shaped neck, seen in flight, identifies all members of this wading family.

Hunting herons space themselves out evenly in favorite hunting spots, and they will strike out suddenly at prey below the water's surface. In flight, their lazy wing beats slowly but effortlessly carry them up to their nests.

These herons nest communally high in trees, building bulky stick nests that are sometimes in plain sight of urban areas. The shallows of coastal estuaries and other, smaller wetlands often produce great numbers of this fascinating year-round resident.

Similar Species: None.

Quick I.D.: very large heron; eagle-sized wingspan; gray-blue plumage; red thighs; long, dagger-like, yellow bill; sexes similar. *In flight:* head folded back; legs held straight back.
Size: 42–50 in.

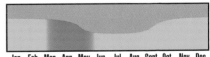

Jan Feb Mar Apr May Jun Jul Aug Sept Oct Nov Dec

Great Egret
Ardea alba

The silky silhouette of the Great Egret graces many marshes, tidal flats and estuaries in the San Diego area. It stalks shallow waters for fish, amphibians and sometimes small birds and mammals. The diligence and patience it displays while hunting contrasts with its lightning-quick, spearing thrust. At dusk, waves of these ghostly birds trace their way back to their communal nesting and roosting sites, which are usually in areas isolated from humans.

From January through late spring, the Great Egret's form is enhanced by the presence of 'nuptial plumes' that flare from its lower neck. Earlier this century, people coveted these feathers for fashion accessories, and Great Egret populations were decimated before legislation was enacted to protect them.

Similar Species: Snowy Egret (p. 28) is smaller and has yellow feet.

breeding

Jan Feb Mar Apr May Jun Jul Aug Sept Oct Nov Dec

Quick I.D.: large heron; all-white plumage; long, yellow bill; black legs and feet; sexes similar. *Breeding:* long white plumes from back and base of neck; green lores.
Size: 36–40 in.

Snowy Egret
Egretta thula

breeding

While all other herons and egrets hunting the shallows of lakes and bays do so in slow, purposeful strides, the Snowy Egret chooses a more energetic approach. It stirs the water with its golden slippers—its black legs are tipped with bright yellow toes that glow in the shallow tidal pools and marshes—to lure small fish, crustaceans and insects into striking range. Should this egret not succeed in its foot-waving foray, it may extend a wing over the open pool to trick fish into swimming toward the shade. Once its prey is within range, the Snowy Egret plucks it from the false haven with the accuracy characteristic of all herons.

Of all the long-legged waders, the Snowy Egret may be the most social nester. Its shallow stick platform is frequently built low in trees. These nesting colonies are vulnerable to human disturbance, and you should keep a respectful distance from them.

Similar Species: Great Egret (p. 27) is larger and has black feet. Cattle Egret (p. 29) has a yellow bill and is smaller. Black-crowned Night-Heron has a black cap and back, a gray neck and gray wings.

Quick I.D.: mid-sized heron; all-white plumage; black bill and legs; yellow feet; yellow lores; sexes similar.
Size: 22–25 in.

Jan Feb Mar Apr May Jun Jul Aug Sept Oct Nov Dec

Cattle Egret
Bubulcus ibis

Cattle Egrets spend most of their days hunched over like tired old-timers. They stand motionless by shorelines and in agricultural area in loose flocks, occasionally eating, but primarily just watching the world go by. Cattle Egrets closely associate with livestock and flooded fields, where they feed on insects, amphibians and worms. They are the most frequently encountered white egrets found far from water.

In spite of their seeming relaxed attitude, however, Cattle Egrets have recently achieved something that no bird has equaled: without the direct influence of humans, Cattle Egrets have colonized much of the North American continent. As recently as the late 1930s, a series of storms carried some of these birds from their native Africa over to the shores of South America. By the 1960s, the relatively graceless egrets had arrived in California, and they now occur in such abundance that it is difficult to imagine our area without them.

Similar Species: Great Egret (p. 27) is larger and has black legs. Snowy Egret (p. 28) has black legs and yellow feet.

non-breeding

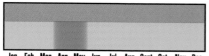

Quick I.D.: snowy-white plumage; yellow-orange bill; yellow legs and feet; sexes similar. *Breeding:* elegant plumes on throat and rump; buff-orange throat, rump and crown; yellow legs and bill turn orange-red; lores may become purple. *Immature:* similar to adult, but with black feet.
Size: 20 in.

Jan Feb Mar Apr May Jun Jul Aug Sept Oct Nov Dec

Sora

Porzana carolina

Skulking around salt- and freshwater marshes in southern California is the seldom-seen Sora. Although this rail arrives from the interior in good numbers in fall, it is not a species that can be encountered with any predictability. Meetings with Soras in southern California arise unexpectedly, usually when birdwatchers are out in good wetlands searching for other more visible species.

The mysterious Sora's breeding status in our area is continually questioned. A small number of these birds are recorded during the summer; however, most of these are thought to be individuals that have not departed for breeding areas. Because of the secrecy of the Sora's life, it is still poorly understood, however, if any of these bachelor birds do indeed pair up and breed in our area. Whatever the local scenario, loads of these wetland tail flickers, breeding elsewhere, arrive in our area in early fall and add greatly to the diversity and interest in our local birding scene.

Similar Species: Virginia Rail has a long, reddish, downcurved bill.

breeding

♂

Quick I.D.: robin sized; short, yellow bill; front of face is black; gray neck and breast; long, greenish legs; sexes similar.
Size: 9–10 in.

Jan Feb Mar Apr May Jun Jul Aug Sept Oct Nov Dec

American Coot

Fulica americana

The American Coot has the lobed toes of a grebe, the bill of a chicken and the body shape and swimming habits of a duck, but it is not remotely related to any of these species: its closest cousins are rails and cranes. American Coots dabble and dive in water and forage on land, and they eat both plant and animal matter. They can be found in just about every freshwater pond, lake, marsh, lagoon or city park in San Diego. They are inland breeders that retreat in great numbers to our mild coastal climates for winter.

These loud, grouchy birds are seen chugging along in wetlands, frequently entering into short-lived disputes with other coots. American Coots appear comical while they swim: their heads bob in time with their paddling feet, and as a coot's swimming speed increases, so does the back-and-forth motion of its head. At peak speed, this motion seems to disorient the coot, and it will run, flap and splash toward the other side of the wetland.

Similar Species: All ducks (pp. 34–43) and grebes (pp. 19–21) generally lack the uniform black color and the white bill.

Jan Feb Mar Apr May Jun Jul Aug Sept Oct Nov Dec

Quick I.D.: smaller than a duck; black body; white bill; red forehead shield; short tail; long legs; lobed feet; white undertail coverts; sexes similar.

Size: 14–16 in.

Brant
Branta bernicla

The local eelgrass beds that spread out along the West Coast are like welcome truck stops for this small, dark marine goose. Thousands of migrating Brant move north in spring along the exposed bars and sandflats of San Diego Bay, on which they feed and preen. Scanning the shorelines along Mission Bay during April will often reveal up to 50 birds fueling up for migration.

Brant, truly geese of the saltwater, migrate exclusively to Alaska along the coast. Brant do not fly in a tight 'V' formation: their flocks fly in wavy lines that frequently alternate between balling up and stretching out. When you encounter a flock along our shorelines in spring, view the bird's delicate, lace-like throat markings and the flock's social behavior from a distance. Disrupting Brant that are feeding or resting often forces the geese to shuffle into the water and to drift away from their important daily activities.

Similar Species: Canada Goose (p. 33) is larger and has white cheeks. Greater White-fronted Goose is brown overall, with dark speckles on its breast. Large ducks lack the black head and long black neck. Cormorants (pp. 23–24) have black bellies and long, slender necks.

Quick I.D.: small goose; dark overall; no white in cheek; faint white 'necklace'; white undertail coverts.
Size: 23–26 in.

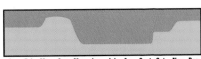

Jan Feb Mar Apr May Jun Jul Aug Sept Oct Nov Dec

Canada Goose

Branta canadensis

Most flocks of Canada Geese in city parks and golf courses show little concern for their human neighbors. These urban geese seem to think nothing of creating a traffic jam, blocking a fairway or dining on lawns and gardens. Breeding pairs mate for life, and not only will a widowed goose occasionally remain unpaired for the rest of its life, it's common for a mate to stay at the side of a fallen partner.

Canada Geese are common along the shores of San Diego Bay and Mission Bay. Many subspecies migrate through California, and they can be recognized by differences in size and color. Most Canada Geese seen around San Diego are of the large race from the Great Basin in eastern California.

Similar Species: Brant (p. 32) and large dabbling ducks are smaller and lack the white cheek. Greater White-fronted Goose lacks the white cheek and the black head and neck.

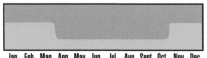

Jan Feb Mar Apr May Jun Jul Aug Sept Oct Nov Dec

Quick I.D.: large goose; white cheek; black head and neck; brown body; white undertail coverts; sexes similar.
Size: 35–43 in.

Mallard
Anas platyrhynchos

The Mallard is the classic duck of inland marshes—the male's iridescent green head and chestnut breast are symbolic of wetland habitat. This large duck is commonly seen feeding in city parks, small lakes and shallow bays. With their legs positioned under the middle part of their bodies, Mallards walk easily, and they can helicopter straight out of water without a running start.

Mallards are the most common duck in North America (and the Northern Hemisphere), and they are easily seen year-round in San Diego. During winter, flocks of Mallards are seen in open freshwater or grazing along shorelines. Because several species often band together in these loose flocks, birdwatchers habitually scan these groups to test their identification skills. Mallards (like all ducks) molt several times a year, so remember that the distinctive green head of the male Mallards occasionally loses its pizzazz.

Similar Species: Male Northern Shoveler (p. 37) has a green head, a white breast and chestnut flanks. Female Mallard resembles many other female dabbling ducks, but look for the blue speculum and her close association with the males.

Quick I.D.: large duck; bright orange feet. *Male:* iridescent green head; bright yellow bill; chestnut breast; white flanks. *Female:* mottled brown; blue speculum bordered by white; bright orange bill marked with black.
Size: 22–26 in.

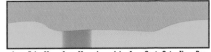

Jan Feb Mar Apr May Jun Jul Aug Sept Oct Nov Dec

Northern Pintail

Anas acuta

As winter frosts bear down upon northern lands, Northern Pintails are driven south to escape the freeze-up. By late November, they have arrived in peak numbers, and they are the most abundant waterfowl in the state. During this time of year, pintails are encountered on lakes, saltwater bays, estuaries and tidal channels, characteristically 'tipping up' and extending their graceful tails skyward.

Northern Pintails breed in small numbers in the San Diego area. The hidden nest sites are often great distances from freshwater marshes and lakes. When the ducklings hatch, the hens may have to march the downy young over a mile to the sanctuary of a wetland.

The Northern Pintail is the most elegant duck to be found in southern California. The male's long, tapering tail feathers and graceful neck contribute to the sleek appearance of this handsome bird.

Similar Species: Mallard (p. 34), American Wigeon (p. 38) and Gadwall are all chunkier and lack the tapered tail.

Jan Feb Mar Apr May Jun Jul Aug Sept Oct Nov Dec

Quick I.D.: large duck; long, slender neck; long, tapered tail; bluish bill. *In flight:* appears slender and sleek.
Male: chocolate-brown head; very long tail; white breast extending up base of neck; dusty gray body. *Female:* mottled light-brown overall.
Size: *Male:* 26–30 in.
Female: 21–23 in.

Cinnamon Teal

Anas cyanoptera

When the morning sun strikes a spring wetland, male Cinnamon Teals glow upon the waters like embers. These handsome ducks are frequently seen swimming along the surface of wetlands, their heads partially submerged, skimming aquatic invertebrates and small seeds from the pond's surface. Often, a series of ducks can be seen following the foraging leader, taking advantage of the sediments the front duck stirs up in the shallows with its paddling feet.

The Cinnamon Teal is one of the few species of ducks that commonly nests in southern California. In a concealed hollow in tall vegetation, occasionally far from water, this teal builds its nest with grass and down. Like many species of ducks, the drab female alone incubates the 7 to 12 eggs for up to 25 days. Mission Bay and other coastal lagoons are favorite nesting places, where females can be seen carefully leading their fluffy ducklings through bulrushes and across small ponds.

Similar Species: Ruddy Duck (p. 43) has a white cheek and a blue bill. Blue-winged Teal lacks the steep forehead.

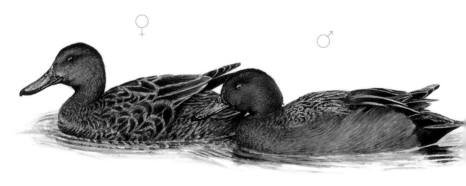

Quick I.D.: small duck.
In flight: blue and green wing patches. *Male:* cinnamon body; red eyes. *Female:* mottled brown overall; broad bill.
Size: 15–16 in.

Jan Feb Mar Apr May Jun Jul Aug Sept Oct Nov Dec

Northern Shoveler
Anas clypeata

The Northern Shoveler's shovel-like bill stands out among dabbling ducks. Its species name—*clypeata*—is Latin for 'furnished with a shield.' The comb-like structures along the bill's edges and its broad, flat shape allow the shoveler to strain small plants and invertebrates from the water's surface or from muddy substrates. A few Northern Shovelers breed in the San Diego area, but most of the shovelers seen in winter reproduce far inland.

Many novice birders become interested in birds because they realize the great variety of ducks in their city parks. Some ducks, like the Northern Shoveler, are dabblers that prefer shallow water, are not opposed to roaming around on land and lift straight off the water like a helicopter. Many other ducks in the San Diego area are divers that are found on large lakes and saltwater bays. They can be seen running across the water to gain enough speed for flight. Separating the divers from the dabblers is a first step into the wondrous world of waterfowl.

Similar Species: Mallard (p. 34) and all other dabbling ducks lack the combination of a large bill, a white breast and chestnut sides.

Jan Feb Mar Apr May Jun Jul Aug Sept Oct Nov Dec

Quick I.D.: mid-sized duck; large bill (longer than head width). *Male:* green head; white breast; chestnut sides. *Female:* mottled brown overall. **Size:** 18–20 in.

American Wigeon
Anas americana

During winter, American Wigeons can easily be found and identified in the shallows and grassy shorelines of San Diego's ponds. From mid-October through April, flocks of wigeons waddle across lawns in parks and golf courses, begging scraps intended for pigeons.

The white top and gray sides of the male American Wigeon's head look somewhat like a balding scalp, while the nasal *wee-he-he-he* calls sound remarkably like the squeaks of a squeezed rubber ducky.

Flocks of American Wigeons, one of our most common North American dabblers, occasionally include some Eurasian Wigeons, their Siberian counterpart. Hundreds of these Asian birds take a wrong turn at the Bering Sea each year and accidentally follow the American shoreline instead of the Asian one during their fall migration.

Similar Species: Eurasian Wigeon (breeds in Asia) has a gold forehead and a cinnamon head without a green swipe. Green-winged Teal is smaller, and has a white shoulder slash and a rusty head with a green swipe.

Quick I.D.: mid-sized duck; cinnamon breast and flanks; white belly; gray bill with black tip; green speculum. *Male:* white forehead; green swipes running back from eyes. *Female:* lacks distinct color on head.
Size: 18–21 in.

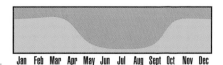

Jan Feb Mar Apr May Jun Jul Aug Sept Oct Nov Dec

Lesser Scaup
Aythya affinis

The Lesser Scaup is the Oreo cookie of the coastal ducks: black at both ends and white in the middle. It is a diving duck that prefers deep, open water, and it is common on lakes, harbors, estuaries and lagoons. As a result of its diving adaptations, the Lesser Scaup is clumsy on land and during take-off, but it gains dignity when it takes to the water. For close-up views, visit the duck-feeding area in various city parks.

Because of San Diego's coastal location, most species of ducks here are of the diving variety, even though the dabblers are often the most frequently encountered. Diving ducks have smaller wings, which helps them dive underwater but makes for difficult take-offs and landings. When a duck scoots across the water in an attempt to get airborne, even a first-time birder can tell it's a diver. Divers' legs are placed well back on their bodies—an advantage for underwater swimming—so in order for diving ducks to stand, they must raise their heavy front ends high to maintain balance.

Similar Species: Greater Scaup has a green tinge to its head and a long white stripe on the trailing edge of its wing (seen in flight), and its head is more rounded. Ring-necked Duck has a white shoulder slash and a black back.

Quick I.D.: peaked head. *Male:* dark head with hints of purple; black breast and hindquarters; dirty white sides; grayish back; blue-gray bill; no white shoulder slash. *Female:* dark brown; well-defined white patch at base of bill.
Size: 15–17 in.

Jan Feb Mar Apr May Jun Jul Aug Sept Oct Nov Dec

Surf Scoter

Melanitta perspicillata

Tough, big and stocky, scoters are more strong than graceful. They are deep-diving sea ducks, and stormy weather amounts to nothing more than a simple annoyance in their feeding habits. Surf Scoters are frequently observed among white-capped waves, and on choppy seas they live up to their name by 'scooting' across the water's surface, occasionally crashing through incoming waves.

Surf Scoters form rafts offshore during the winter months. They dive to wrench shellfish from rocks with their sturdy bills, and they swallow the shellfish whole. In spring, these large black ducks migrate to lakes and tundra ponds as far north as Alaska and the Yukon.

Similar Species: White-winged Scoter has white wing patches, and the male has white eye spots. Male Black Scoter is all-black, and the female has a white face and throat. Other dark waterfowl lack the white forehead and nape.

Quick I.D.: large duck.
Male: black overall; white forehead, nape and base of bill; orange bill. *Female:* dark brown; light cheek.
Size: 18–21 in.

Jan Feb Mar Apr May Jun Jul Aug Sept Oct Nov Dec

Bufflehead
Bucephala albeola

The small, fluffy Bufflehead is perhaps the 'cutest' of our ducks: its simple plumage and rotund physique bring to mind a child's stuffed toy. During winter, it is found on just about every lake, pond and wetland in the area. Although common in parks and urban ponds, baby-faced Buffleheads (unlike many other duck species) rarely accept handouts from humans.

Because ducks spend most of their lives dripping with water, preening is an important behavior. At the base of the tail of most birds lies the preen (uropygial) gland, which secretes a viscous liquid that inhibits bacterial growth and waterproofs and conditions the feathers. After gently squeezing the preen gland with its bill, a bird can spread the secretion methodically over most of its body, an essential practice to revitalize precious feathers. Since sun and wind damage feathers, it is understandable that birds spend so much time preening and conditioning their feathers.

Similar Species: Male Common Goldeneye, Barrow's Goldeneye and Hooded Merganser are all larger and lack the white, unbordered triangles behind the eyes.

Jan Feb Mar Apr May Jun Jul Aug Sept Oct Nov Dec

Quick I.D.: tiny duck; round body. *Male:* white triangles on back of dark head; white body; dark back. *Female:* dirty brown; small white cheek patch.
Size: 13–15 in.

Red-breasted Merganser
Mergus serrator

The Red-breasted Merganser runs along the surface of the water, beating its heavy wings, to build up sufficient speed for lift-off. Once in the air, this large duck looks compressed and arrow-like as it flies strongly in low, straight lines. Mergansers are lean and powerful waterfowl adapted to the underwater pursuit of fish. Unlike other fishing birds, a merganser has a saw-like bill that is serrated to ensure that squirmy, slimy prey do not escape.

Red-breasted Mergansers are found almost exclusively on saltwater during winter. Their quick 'fly bys,' which flash white inner wing patches, are more common winter features than a look at their crazed, punk-like 'hairstyles.'

Similar Species: Male Common Merganser (rare in San Diego) lacks the red breast and has white underparts, and the female has a well-defined, reddish-brown hood. Other large ducks and Common Loon all lack the combination of a green head, an orange bill, orange feet and a red breast.

Quick I.D.: large duck; gray body. *Male:* well-defined, dark green hood; punk-like crest; spotted, red breast; white collar; brilliant orange bill and feet; black spinal streak. *Female:* rusty hood blending into white breast.
Size: 21–25 in.

Jan Feb Mar Apr May Jun Jul Aug Sept Oct Nov Dec

Ruddy Duck
Oxyura jamaicensis

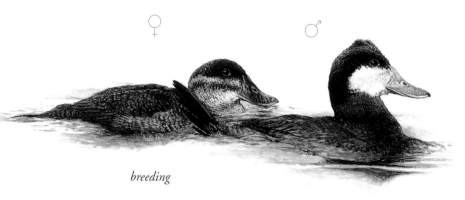

breeding

The clowns of freshwater wetlands, male Ruddy Ducks energetically paddle around their breeding wetlands, displaying with great vigor and beating their breasts with their bright blue beaks. The *plap-plap-plap-plap-plap* sound of their display speeds up until its climax: a spasmodic jerk and sputter. The male's performance occurs from May to the middle of June.

The Ruddy Duck's winter demeanor contrasts sharply with its summer habits. The drably plumaged males lack their courting energy and their summer colors. These stiff-tailed diving ducks are found commonly during the non-breeding season offshore at San Diego Bay and Mission Bay.

Similar Species: All other waterfowl are generally larger and have shorter tails and relatively smaller heads.

Quick I.D.: small duck; broad bill; large head; tail often cocked up. *Breeding male:* reddish-brown neck and body; black head and tail; white cheek; blue bill. *Non-breeding male:* dull brown overall; dark cap; white cheek. *Female:* like non-breeding male, but pale cheek has a dark stripe.
Size: 14–16 in.

Jan Feb Mar Apr May Jun Jul Aug Sept Oct Nov Dec

Turkey Vulture
Cathartes aura

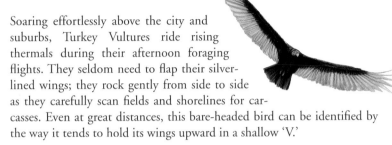

Soaring effortlessly above the city and suburbs, Turkey Vultures ride rising thermals during their afternoon foraging flights. They seldom need to flap their silver-lined wings; they rock gently from side to side as they carefully scan fields and shorelines for carcasses. Even at great distances, this bare-headed bird can be identified by the way it tends to hold its wings upward in a shallow 'V.'

The Turkey Vulture feeds entirely on carrion, which it can sometimes detect by scent alone. Its head is featherless, which is an adaptation to staying clean and parasite-free while it digs around inside carcasses. The Turkey Vulture's well-known habit of regurgitating its rotting meal at intruders may be a defense mechanism: it allows adults to reduce their weight for quicker take-off, and its smell helps young vultures repel would-be predators.

Similar Species: Hawks (pp. 47–49), eagles and Osprey all have large, feathered heads and tend to hold their wings flatter in flight, not in a shallow 'V.'

Quick I.D.: larger than a hawk; all-black; small red head; sexes similar. *In flight:* wings held in a shallow 'V'; silver-gray flight feathers; dark wing linings.
Size: 27–30 in.

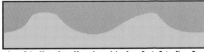

Jan Feb Mar Apr May Jun Jul Aug Sept Oct Nov Dec

White-tailed Kite
Elanus leucurus

The White-tailed Kite flies with unusual grace and buoyancy for a raptor. It normally hunts during dawn and dusk, when it can be found hovering over rolling hills, wet meadows and cultivated fields. The population of this regal bird (formerly known as the Black-shouldered Kite) appears to have stabilized recently, after serious declines caused by egg collectors, habitat loss and unwarranted shootings.

The White-tailed Kite nests in trees and tall bushes in semi-open areas. The nests are often built near the treetop, away from the main trunk and horizontal limbs. During incubation and after hatching, the male kite diligently provides the growing family with steady feasts of small rodents, which he catches in prime habitats near the nest. When the White-tailed Kite spots a vole wandering through the grass, it parachutes down on the rodent, with its wings held high.

Similar Species: Hawks (pp. 47–49) and falcons lack the pure-white tail and black shoulders. Male Northern Harrier (p. 46) lacks the black shoulders and has a conspicuous white rump.

Quick I.D.: small hawk–sized; long white tail; pointed wings; black shoulders; gray back; sexes similar. *In flight:* frequently hovers.
Size: 15–17 in.

Jan Feb Mar Apr May Jun Jul Aug Sept Oct Nov Dec

Northern Harrier
Circus cyaneus

This common marsh hawk can best be identified by its flight behavior: the Northern Harrier follows wavy lines over lush meadows, often retracing its path several times in the quest for prey. Watch the slow, lazy wing beats of the Northern Harrier coincide with its undulating, erratic flight pattern as this raptor skims the brambles and bulrushes with its belly. Unlike other hawks, which can find their prey only visually, the Northern Harrier stays close enough to the ground to listen for birds, voles and mice. When movement catches the harrier's eyes or ears, it abandons its lazy ways to strike at its prey with channeled energy.

The Northern Harrier is a common winter visitor and a rare breeder in the San Diego area. This species is often called the Marsh Hawk, and the draining of area marshes have led to a decline in its numbers.

Similar Species: Hawks (pp. 47–49) and Short-eared Owl all lack the white rump.

Quick I.D.: mid-sized hawk; white rump; long tail; long wings; owl-like face (seen only at close range). *Male:* grayish upperparts; whitish underparts; black wing tips. *Female* and *Immature:* brown overall.
Size: 18–22 in.

Jan Feb Mar Apr May Jun Jul Aug Sept Oct Nov Dec

Sharp-shinned Hawk

Accipiter striatus

If songbirds dream, the Sharp-shinned Hawk is sure to be the source of their nightmares. 'Sharpies' pursue small birds through forests, maneuvering around limbs and branches in the hope of acquiring prey. Sharp-shinned Hawks take many birds, with small songbirds and the occasional woodpecker being the most numerous items.

During the winter months, many of San Diego's neighborhoods have a resident Sharp-shinned Hawk, eager to capture unwary finches, sparrows and starlings. Backyard feeders tend to concentrate songbirds, so they are attractive foraging areas for this small hawk. A sudden eruption of songbirds off the feeder and a few feathers floating on the wind are often the signs of a sudden, successful Sharp-shinned attack.

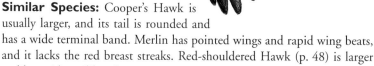

Similar Species: Cooper's Hawk is usually larger, and its tail is rounded and has a wide terminal band. Merlin has pointed wings and rapid wing beats, and it lacks the red breast streaks. Red-shouldered Hawk (p. 48) is larger and has wider tail bands.

Quick I.D.: pigeon-sized; short, round wings; long tail; blue-gray back; red horizontal streaking on underparts; red eyes. *In flight:* flap-and-glide flier; heavily barred tail has squared tip. *Immature:* brown overall; vertical, brown streaks on breast; yellow eyes.

Size: 12–14 in. (female larger).

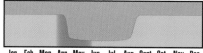

Jan Feb Mar Apr May Jun Jul Aug Sept Oct Nov Dec

Red-shouldered Hawk
Buteo lineatus

Unlike many other hawks in the San Diego area, the Red-shouldered Hawk does most of its hunting from a perch. Sitting atop a fencepost, utility pole or tree, this small, intricately colored raptor waits patiently above a lake or wet meadow. From its vantage point, it uses keen eyes and sharp ears to detect frogs, toads, snakes, mice and occasionally crayfish or other invertebrates.

The Red-shouldered Hawk nests in mature trees, usually in oaks and riparian growth, and the stick nest is built in a crotch. As spring approaches and pair bonds are formed and reinforced, the normally docile hawks utter loud and shrieking *kee-you kee-you kee-you* calls.

Similar Species: Sharp-shinned Hawk (p. 47) and Cooper's Hawk have longer, narrower tails and lack the rufous shoulders. Red-tailed Hawk (p. 49) is larger and lacks the tail banding.

Quick I.D.: mid-sized hawk; heavily banded tail; red wing linings; dark rufous breast with white, horizontal streaks; sexes similar.
Size: 18–22 in.

Jan Feb Mar Apr May Jun Jul Aug Sept Oct Nov Dec

Red-tailed Hawk

Buteo jamaicensis

With its fierce facial expression and untidy feathers, the Red-tailed Hawk looks as though it has been suddenly and rudely awakened. Its characteristic scream further suggests that the Red-tailed Hawk is a bird best avoided. You would think other birds would treat this large raptor with more respect, but the Red-tailed Hawk is constantly being harassed by crows, jays and blackbirds.

Until this hawk is two or three years old, its tail is brown, not brick red; the dark head, the black 'belt' around the midsection and the dark leading edge to its wings are better field marks because they're seen in most Red-tails. It's hard not to spot a Red-tail perched on a post or soaring lazily overhead along most freeways, highways and byways passing through open country.

Similar Species: Northern Harrier (p. 46) has a white rump. Sharp-shinned Hawk (p. 47) and Cooper's Hawk are smaller, have long tails and rarely soar. Red-shouldered Hawk (p. 48) is smaller and has broad, dark tail bands. Rough-legged Hawk (rare winter migrant) has distinctive elbow patches.

Jan Feb Mar Apr May Jun Jul Aug Sept Oct Nov Dec

Quick I.D.: large hawk; brick-red tail (adult only); dark head; thin brown belt; light flight feathers; dark wing lining; sexes similar.
Size: 20–23 in.

American Kestrel

Falco sparverius

This small, noisy falcon is a common summer sight over much of California. It has adapted well to rural life, and it is commonly seen perched on power lines, watching for unwary grasshoppers, birds and rodents. When not perched, American Kestrels can often be seen hovering above potential prey. All falcons are skilled hunters, and they have a unique, tooth-like projection on their hooked bills that can quickly crush the neck of small prey. The American Kestrel's species name *sparverius* is Latin for 'pertaining to sparrows,' an occasional prey item.

The nests of American Kestrels are often built in abandoned woodpecker cavities. Conservationists have recently discovered that kestrels will use nest boxes when natural cavities are unavailable, which should ensure that these active predators remain common throughout our area.

Similar Species: Sharp-shinned Hawk (p. 47) and Cooper's Hawk have short, rounder wings. Merlin is larger, has a banded tail and lacks the facial stripes.

Quick I.D.: jay-sized; long, pointed wings; long tail; two vertical, black stripes on face; spotted breast; hooked bill. *In flight:* rapid wing beat. *Male:* blue wings; russet back; colorful head. *Female:* russet back and wings.
Size: 8–10 in.

Jan	Feb	Mar	Apr	May	Jun	Jul	Aug	Sept	Oct	Nov	Dec

California Quail
Callipepla californica

With its distinctive, forward-facing plume, the California Quail looks like a flapper from the 1920s. California Quails scuttle around in tight, cohesive groups, and in fall and winter, these coveys can include up to 200 birds.

In chaparral and suburban gardens, quail coveys have succumbed to predation by released feral cats, but they are still often seen darting across paths in search of dense cover. Even when these shy birds refuse to leave their shrubby sanctuary, their noisy scratching and soft vocalizations betray their presence. During April and May, listen as the males advertise their courting desires by characteristically uttering *where are you?*

Similar Species: None.

Quick I.D.: robin-sized; forward-facing plume; gray-brown back; gray breast; white scales on belly; unfeathered legs. *Male:* black throat; white stripes on head and neck. *Female:* gray-brown face and throat.
Size: 10 in.

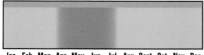

Jan Feb Mar Apr May Jun Jul Aug Sept Oct Nov Dec

Black-bellied Plover

Pluvialis squatarola

During winter, Black-bellied Plovers are commonly seen darting along sea beaches, grassy openings and ploughed fields, foraging with a robin-like run-and-stop technique. Although they dress in plain grays for much of their San Diego retreat, many Black-bellied Plovers can be seen in their summer tuxedo plumage in early spring and late fall.

Not all walks on the beach will bring an encounter with a plover, but a keen observer can determine if one was strolling the sand earlier. The Black-bellied Plover lacks a hind digit and leaves a three-toed print, whereas most other sandpipers that overwinter on the coast have four toes.

Similar Species: Willet (p. 57) is larger and has a longer bill. Other shorebirds are neither as plump nor as gray.

non-breeding

Quick I.D.: larger than a robin; short, stout, black bill; relatively long, dark legs; sexes similar. *Non-breeding:* slightly streaked, gray body. *In flight:* black wing pits; white rump; white wing linings.
Size: 11–12 in.

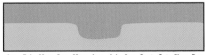

Jan Feb Mar Apr May Jun Jul Aug Sept Oct Nov Dec

Snowy Plover
Charadrius alexandrinus

The Snowy Plover is an inconspicuous year-round patron of some of our more remote beaches. Blending gracefully with the soft brown sands, this small shorebird moves ghost-like over isolated dunes and open beaches. Snowy Plovers were at one time found all along the coastline, but development and disturbance now restrict this species to a few protected areas.

Although it may be tempting to search for Snowy Plovers, this activity is likely not in the best interest of the bird. Its nesting activities can easily be disrupted by good-intentioned birdwatchers who inadvertently scare the parent bird away from its nest for prolonged periods. In addition, the bird's nest is difficult to spot and can quite easily be crushed under a negligent foot. For these reasons Snowies should only be sought out in the non-breeding season, when human disturbances are minimized and their population is boosted by the arrival of inland nesters that have retreated to the coast for the winter.

Similar Species: Semipalmated Plover has a darker back, a complete breast band and a bicolored bill. Killdeer (p. 54) has two black breast bands and is much larger.

Quick I.D.: smaller than a robin; white underparts; light brown upperparts; thin, black bill; sexes similar. *Adult:* dark patches on ear, shoulder and forehead; slate-gray legs. *Juvenile:* lacks dark patches.

Size: 6¹/₂ in.

Jan Feb Mar Apr May Jun Jul Aug Sept Oct Nov Dec

Killdeer

Charadrius vociferus

The Killdeer is probably the most widespread shorebird in California. It nests on gravelly shorelines, utility rights-of-way, lawns, pastures and occasionally on gravel roofs within cities. Its name is a paraphrase of its distinctive, loud call: *kill-dee kill-dee kill-deer.*

The Killdeer's response to predators relies on deception and good acting skills. To divert a predator's attention away from a nest or a brood of young, an adult Killdeer (like many shorebirds) will flop around to feign an injury (usually a broken wing or leg). Once the Killdeer has the attention of the fox, crow or gull, it leads the predator away from the vulnerable nest. After it reaches a safe distance, the adult Killdeer is suddenly 'healed' and flies off, leaving the predator without a meal.

Similar Species: Semipalmated Plover has only one breast band, is smaller and is found only on mudflats.

Quick I.D.: robin-sized; two black breast bands; brown back; russet rump; long legs; white underparts; sexes similar.
Size: 9–11 in.

Jan Feb Mar Apr May Jun Jul Aug Sept Oct Nov Dec

Black-necked Stilt

Himantopus mexicanus

On long, gangly legs, the Black-necked Stilt strides daintily through shallow pools, brackish ponds and salt evaporators. Its grace, beauty and fragility are highlights in sometimes desolate and unassuming habitats. Purposeful in each stride, stilts walk and peck at the moist substrate and at the water's surface with their long needle-like bill. These shorebirds eat a variety of waterbugs, waterbeetles and small crustaceans, which they catch with pinpoint accuracy. Males tend to be slightly larger, darker and longer-legged than females, and they forage in deeper water, which reduces the competition for food.

Similar Species: American Avocet (p. 56) lacks the black crown and has an upcurved bill and baby blue legs. Black Oystercatcher is all-black and has a red bill.

Jan Feb Mar Apr May Jun Jul Aug Sept Oct Nov Dec

Quick I.D.: larger than a pigeon; very long, pinkish (red) legs; dark upperparts; clean white underparts; long, straight, needle-like, black bill; small white eyebrow; sexes similar (but male has slightly blacker upperparts).
Size: 13$^1/_2$–15$^1/_2$ in.

American Avocet
Recurvirostra americana

Even in its subdued winter plumage, the American Avocet, with its grace-ful upturned bill and long, baby-blue legs, is one of the most elegant in-habitants of the San Diego area. In flight, its long legs and bill help make this slim bird look like a winged stick.

One of the common ways the American Avocet forages is by sweeping its bill quickly from side to side, just below the water's surface. Despite the whip-like quickness of this action, it is surprisingly effective at collecting tiny invertebrates suspended in the water. The American Avocet also uses a duck-like, tipped-up feeding behavior while swimming. It uses its par-tially webbed feet to negotiate areas of deep water.

Similar Species: Willet (p. 57) lacks the long bill and the long, trailing legs in flight. Black-necked Stilt (p. 55) lacks the upturned bill and has black extending from its crown to its back.

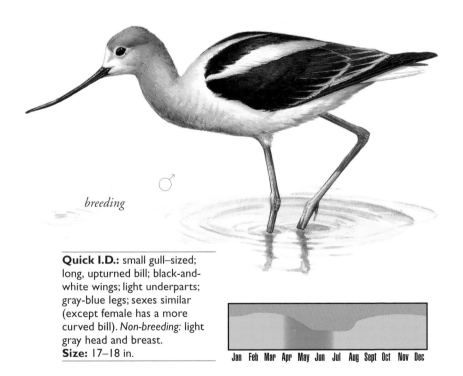

♂

breeding

Quick I.D.: small gull–sized; long, upturned bill; black-and-white wings; light underparts; gray-blue legs; sexes similar (except female has a more curved bill). *Non-breeding*: light gray head and breast.
Size: 17–18 in.

Jan Feb Mar Apr May Jun Jul Aug Sept Oct Nov Dec

Willet

Catoptrophorus semipalmatus

On the exposed mudflats at Mission Bay, masses of shorebirds concentrate during migration and winter. Although these birds are among the most difficult birds to identify in isolation, shorebirds here reward the birdwatcher with the luxury of comparison.

These large, gray-brown sandpipers can be seen on tidal flats, along sandy and rocky shorelines and in most wetlands. Foraging Willets can be confusing to beginning birdwatchers because resting birds have few diagnostic field marks and their winter plumage is dull. When Willets take wing, however, their flight feathers and wing linings are an unmistakable clash of black and white as they move from one foraging site to another. The call of this common shorebird is easily recognized. It sounds like a musical *will-will-willet will-willet.*

Similar Species: Greater Yellowlegs and Lesser Yellowlegs have yellow legs and a fine bill. Whimbrel (p. 58), Marbled Godwit (p. 59), Short-billed Dowitcher (p. 65) and Long-billed Dowitcher all lack the black-and-white wing patterning.

non-breeding

| Jan | Feb | Mar | Apr | May | Jun | Jul | Aug | Sept | Oct | Nov | Dec |

Quick I.D.: larger than a pigeon; plump; gray; sexes similar. *Non-breeding:* black-and-white wing patterning; dark, heavy bill; gray legs.
Size: 14–16 in.

Whimbrel

Numenius phaeopus

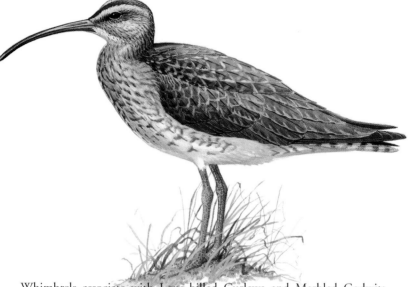

Whimbrels associate with Long-billed Curlews and Marbled Godwits, and one wonders how their identity can ever be confusing. Size and subtle differences are obvious here as one stands a few yards from these winter visitors. The Whimbrel plunges its decurved bill into the soft substrate to forage at mid-depth, deeper than the Dunlin but nowhere near the range of the curlew.

Most shorebirds in San Diego dine on the rich invertebrate life in the fertile tidal flats. Whimbrels, which sweep through our area, connect our mudflats with those throughout our hemisphere. True trans-continental citizens, San Diego's Whimbrels may nest in the northern tundra and winter as far south as Chile. The airy pronunciation of the word 'whimbrel' seems to echo perfectly this wind birds' mastery of flight; the true derivation of its name, however, is from a modification of its call.

Similar Species: Long-billed Curlew is larger and lacks the striped crown. Marbled Godwit (p. 59) lacks the downcurved bill.

Quick I.D.: large shorebird; long, downcurved bill; striped crown; dark eye line; mottled brown body; sexes similar.
Size: 15–18 in.

Jan Feb Mar Apr May Jun Jul Aug Sept Oct Nov Dec

Marbled Godwit

Limosa fedoa

The lance-like bill of the Marbled Godwit may look plenty long enough to reach buried worms, amphipods and small clams, but the godwit doesn't seem content with its reach. It is frequently seen foraging with its head submerged beneath the water's surface or with its face pressed against the mud. The deep probes seem to satisfy this large shorebird: godwits look genuinely pleased with a face full of mud!

The Marbled Godwit's bill is two-toned—light near the face and dark at the tip. The dark tip may give the bill extra strength, because black pigments are stronger than light-colored pigments. The Marbled Godwit's voice is a loud squawking cry, rising above other mudflat specialists. Although simple, the call is easily remembered as the bird barks out its name: *God-wit God-wit.*

Similar Species: Long-billed Curlew and Whimbrel (p. 58) have downcurved bills. Willet (p. 57) has black-and-white wings and a shorter bill. Short-billed Dowitcher (p. 65) and Long-billed Dowitcher have straight, dark bills.

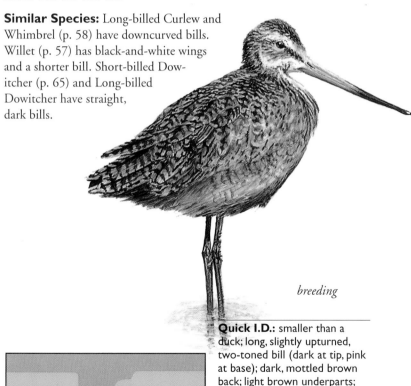

breeding

Quick I.D.: smaller than a duck; long, slightly upturned, two-toned bill (dark at tip, pink at base); dark, mottled brown back; light brown underparts; sexes similar.

Size: 17–19 in.

Jan Feb Mar Apr May Jun Jul Aug Sept Oct Nov Dec

Black Turnstone

Arenaria melanocephala

During migration and in winter, Black Turnstones live on barnacle- and seaweed-covered rocky outcrops. They can often be seen on reefs, breakwaters and rocky beaches throughout our area. Turnstones probe the nooks and crevices on the wave-splashed rocks for amphipods, isopods and other small invertebrates that live hidden along the tide line.

Black Turnstones do much of their foraging by probing, but they have gained fame for an unusual feeding technique. As the name implies, the turnstone flips over small rocks and ocean debris with its bill to expose hidden invertebrates. The turnstone's bill is short, stubby and slightly up-turned—ideal for this foraging style.

Similar Species: Ruddy Turnstone has rust color in its wings and back. Surfbird has yellowish-green legs and a terminal black band on its white tail. Wandering Tattler teeters and bobs as it feeds, and is light gray and larger.

non-breeding

Quick I.D.: robin-sized; white belly; dark reddish-brown legs; stout, slightly upturned bill; sexes similar. *Breeding:* black upperparts; white eyebrow and lore spot. *Non-breeding:* dark brownish-gray upperparts.
Size: 9 in.

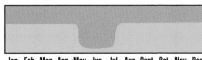

Jan Feb Mar Apr May Jun Jul Aug Sept Oct Nov Dec

Sanderling
Calidris alba

A winter stroll along a sandy saltwater beach is occasionally punctuated by the sight of these tiny runners. They appear to enjoy nothing more than playing in the surf. Sanderlings are characteristically seen chasing and retreating from the rolling waves, never getting caught in the surf. Only the Sanderling commonly forages in this manner, plucking at the exposed invertebrates stirred up by the wave action. Without waves to chase along calm shorelines, Sanderlings daintily probe into wet soil in much the same fashion as many other sandpipers.

This sandpiper species is one of the world's most widespread birds. It breeds across the Arctic in Alaska, Canada and Russia, and it spends winter running up and down sandy shorelines in North America, South America, Asia, Africa and Australia.

Similar Species: Western Sandpiper (p. 62) and Least Sandpiper (p. 63) are smaller and darker. Dunlin (p. 64) is darker and has a downcurved bill.

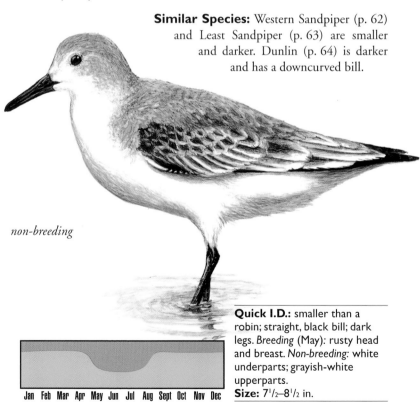

non-breeding

Jan Feb Mar Apr May Jun Jul Aug Sept Oct Nov Dec

Quick I.D.: smaller than a robin; straight, black bill; dark legs. *Breeding* (May): rusty head and breast. *Non-breeding*: white underparts; grayish-white upperparts.
Size: 7¹/₂–8¹/₂ in.

Western Sandpiper

Calidris mauri

non-breeding

Wintering Western Sandpipers look nondescript, but what they lack in defining plumage they make up for in numbers and synchrony. At migration times in fall and spring, thousands of these shorebirds huddle and forage along open mudflats, picking at the tiny organisms that live in the damp shorelines.

The challenge of identifying wintering shorebirds awaits the interested birder. From July through September, many species of these confusing 'peeps' (as they are collectively called by birders) can be observed with patience and at very close range. Even if the subtlety of plumage is not your primary interest, a morning spent with shuffling sandpipers will prove to be enjoyable.

Similar Species: Sanderling (p. 61) is larger and frequently runs in the surf. Least Sandpiper (p. 63) is smaller and has pale legs. Dunlin (p. 64) is larger and has more brown on its head.

Quick I.D.: larger than a sparrow; black legs and bill. *Breeding:* rusty patches on crown, cheek and wings. *Non-breeding:* grayish upperparts; white breast.
Size: 6–7 in.

Jan Feb Mar Apr May Jun Jul Aug Sept Oct Nov Dec

Least Sandpiper
Calidris minutilla

The Least Sandpiper is the smallest of the shorebirds, but its size is not a deterrent to its migratory feats. Like most other 'peeps'—a term used to group the nearly indistinguishable *Calidris* sandpipers—the Least Sandpipers that winter in southern California migrate to the Arctic to breed.

Groups of these tiny birds can be spotted against the damp sands of beaches, mudflats and lakeshores throughout our area. Their plumage matches perfectly their preferred habitat, as it is usually their rapid movements that reveal these diminutive sprinters. Least Sandpipers tenaciously peck the moist substrate with their dexterous bill, eating mosquitoes, beach fleas, amphipods and other aquatic invertebrates.

Similar Species: Pectoral Sandpiper is larger and has a well-defined pectoral border. Other 'peeps' (pp. 61–64) all tend to have dark legs and are generally larger.

non-breeding

Quick I.D.: sexes similar. *Adult:* black bill; yellow legs; dark, mottled back; buff-brown breast, head and nape; light breast streaking. *Immature:* like adult, but with faintly streaked breast.
Size: 6 in.

Jan Feb Mar Apr May Jun Jul Aug Sept Oct Nov Dec

Dunlin

Calidris alpina

Flocks of these birds can occasionally be seen on both fresh- and saltwater shorelines. The flocks move about continuously at San Diego Bay and Mission Bay, where there are often dozens of Dunlins through winter. These tight flocks are generally more exclusive than many other shorebird troupes: few shorebird species mix with groups of Dunlins.

The Dunlin, like most other shorebirds, nests on the arctic tundra and winters on the coasts of North America, Europe and Asia. It was originally called a 'Dunling' (meaning 'a small brown bird'), but for unknown reasons the 'g' was later dropped.

Similar Species: Sanderling (p. 61) is paler and is usually seen running in the surf. Western Sandpiper (p. 62) and Least Sandpiper (p. 63) are smaller.

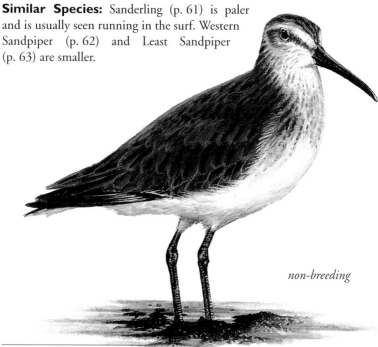

non-breeding

Quick I.D.: smaller than a robin; slightly downcurved bill; dark legs. *Breeding* (April–May): black belly; streaked underparts; rusty back. *Non-breeding:* pale gray underparts; grayish-brown upperparts.
Size: 8–9 in.

Jan Feb Mar Apr May Jun Jul Aug Sept Oct Nov Dec

Short-billed Dowitcher
Limnodromus griseus

When winter tides are at their highest, shorebirds concentrate in large numbers along mudflats and estuaries in the San Diego area. High tides force dowitchers and other wintering shorebirds to high, dry ground, often packing them together in large numbers. There they are easily identified, because dowitchers tend to be stockier than most shorebirds, and they avoid deeper water.

The sewing machine–like rhythms that dowitchers perform while foraging deeply into the mudflats is helpful for distinguishing them from other shorebirds. Separating the two dowitcher species, however, is one of the most difficult tasks any birder may attempt. Although most people are perfectly content to simply call them 'dowitchers,' some birders can separate the two species, which are extremely similar in winter plumage, by their voice.

Similar Species: Long-billed Dowitcher has barring on its sides and an unmarked breast, its plumage is darker overall, and its bill is slightly longer. Common Snipe (p. 66) has longer legs, heavily barred upperparts and different foraging techniques.

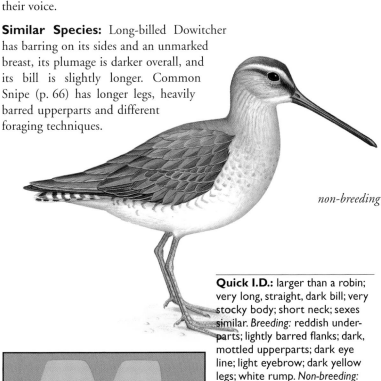

non-breeding

Quick I.D.: larger than a robin; very long, straight, dark bill; very stocky body; short neck; sexes similar. *Breeding:* reddish underparts; lightly barred flanks; dark, mottled upperparts; dark eye line; light eyebrow; dark yellow legs; white rump. *Non-breeding:* gray overall; white belly.
Size: 11–12½ in. (female larger).

Jan Feb Mar Apr May Jun Jul Aug Sept Oct Nov Dec

Common Snipe
Gallinago gallinago

Common Snipes have startled many walkers as they stroll through local marshes. These shorebirds are both secretive and well camouflaged, so few people notice them until the birds fly suddenly out from nearby grassy tussocks. As soon as a snipe takes to the air, it performs a series of quick zigzags, an evasive maneuver designed to confuse predators. Snipes are seldom seen in large groups, nor are they normally encountered along open shorelines; their heavily streaked plumage is suited to grassy habitat.

Because snipes do not commonly nest in the San Diego area, it is always a special treat when a spring or fall bird is heard 'winnowing.' This mystical sound, produced in flight by air passing through spread tail feathers, is heard only periodically, but often enough so that the thrill of each experience is never lost.

Similar Species: All other shorebirds are either too short of bill or not as heavily streaked.

Quick I.D.: robin-sized; long, black-tipped bill; heavily streaked back; short neck; striped head; long legs; sexes similar.
Size: 10¹/₂–11¹/₂ in.

Jan	Feb	Mar	Apr	May	Jun	Jul	Aug	Sept	Oct	Nov	Dec

Red-necked Phalarope
Phalaropus lobatus

Red-necked Phalaropes spin and whirl in open water during their migratory stopovers in San Diego, displaying an unexpected foraging technique for a shorebird. These small shorebirds land on the water and swim in tight circles, stirring up tiny crustaceans and quickly picking at the water's surface with their needle-like bills.

Not only do Red-necked Phalaropes display unusual feeding strategies, but these most colorful of the spring shorebirds also exhibit breeding habits that are extremely rare through the entire animal kingdom. On their tundra nesting grounds, these migrants practice a mating strategy known as polyandry—the females mate with several males. The more brightly colored female phalarope defends the nest site from other females, and it is her mate who incubates the eggs and rears the young.

Similar Species: Wilson's Phalarope (summer visitor) has a lighter head and back and unspotted flanks.

non-breeding

Jan Feb Mar Apr May Jun Jul Aug Sept Oct Nov Dec

Quick I.D.: robin-sized; thin, black bill; long, black legs; white wing stripe. *Breeding female:* chestnut neck and throat; white chin; blue-black head; incomplete, white eye ring; white belly; buff stripes on upper wings; spotted flanks. *Breeding male:* white eyebrow; less intense colors. *Non-breeding:* white underparts; gray-blue upperparts; black mask extends from eyes; white streaks on back.
Size: 7–8 in.

Bonaparte's Gull
Larus philadelphia

non-breeding

The scratchy little calls of Bonaparte's Gulls can be heard as these winter residents forage along the waterfront. These gulls commonly feed on the water's surface, and they can often be seen resting atop concrete diving platforms. After spending the winter months here, most Bonaparte's Gulls leave the coast for the summer to breed in the northern boreal forest, where they nest, in most un–gull-like fashion, in spruce trees.

Outside the summer breeding season, most Bonaparte's Gulls lose their distinctive black hoods, but they retain flashy white wing patches and a noticeable black ear spot behind the eyes.

This gull was named not after the famed French emperor, but after his nephew, Charles Lucien Bonaparte, who brought recognition to his family's name through the practice of ornithology.

Similar Species: Mew Gull lacks the black ear spot and is larger. Forster's Tern (p. 75) has a forked tail and lacks the white wing flash.

Quick I.D.: small gull; black bill; dark eyes; wing tips have black outline; wings flash white in flight; sexes similar. *Breeding:* black hood. *Non-breeding:* white head with a dark ear spot.
Size: 12–14 in.

Jan Feb Mar Apr May Jun Jul Aug Sept Oct Nov Dec

Heermann's Gull

Larus heermanni

While most novice birdwatchers struggle with the identification of gulls, southern Californians are blessed with the handsome Heermann's Gull. Whether clad in its adult or immature wardrobe, this West Coast gull is North America's most distinctive.

Although most gulls migrate north to breed and then return south, the Heermann's is an exception. After raising its chicks on sun-baked Isla Rasa in the Gulf of California, Heermann's Gulls are drawn northward. Although we are fortunate to have these birds year-round, they are most easily seen from fall through spring, along rocky cliffs, offshore waters and sea beaches.

Patiently follow a flock of Heermann's Gulls in the presence of Brown Pelicans and cormorants, and you will see the gulls habitually annoy the larger birds in the hopes of snatching unguarded prey remains.

Similar Species: Juvenile California Gull (p. 71) is larger and has a mottled brown body.

non-breeding

Quick I.D.: small gull; sexes similar. *Adult:* red bill; ashy-gray body; white head; white-tipped, black tail. *Immature:* soft brown body; dark legs.
Size: 16–18 in.

Jan Feb Mar Apr May Jun Jul Aug Sept Oct Nov Dec

Ring-billed Gull
Larus delawarensis

As August rolls through our area, Ring-billed Gulls return from their nesting sites in the Great Basin to overwinter along the coast. These mid-sized gulls do not make up a majority of the gull flocks in San Diego, but their bills are sufficiently distinctive to set them apart from the more numerous species in the area. The black ring around both the upper and lower mandible does not reach the bill's tip, which is as yellow as the rest of the bill.

During winter, Ring-billed Gulls can be encountered throughout the San Diego area. They associate with other flocks of gulls in city parks, in shopping center parking lots, near fastfood restaurants and on lakes and ponds. Along beaches, Ring-billed Gulls eat dead fish, birds and other animal matter, while inland they take worms, garbage and waste grain.

Similar Species: No other gull has a ring around its bill. Heermann's Gull (p. 69) is darker and has a red bill. Glaucous-winged Gull is much larger and has dark eyes, pink legs and gray wing tips. Mew Gull has dark eyes. Herring Gull is larger and has pink legs. California Gull (p. 71) is larger and has dark eyes.

non-breeding

Quick I.D.: mid-sized gull; black ring near bill tip; yellow bill and legs; dark gray wing covers; light eyes; black wing tips; small white spots on black primaries; white underparts; sexes similar. *Non-breeding:* white head and nape washed with brown. *First winter:* mottled grayish brown; gray back; blackish-brown primaries; brown band on tail.
Size: 18–20 in.

Jan Feb Mar Apr May Jun Jul Aug Sept Oct Nov Dec

California Gull
Larus californicus

California Gulls leave their inland breeding grounds to trickle back to the coast starting in late June. Most of them have arrived by August and will stay for the following eight months. California Gulls winter exclusively on the West Coast, from the Pacific Northwest down through Baja California.

When at their breeding grounds on the plains, California Gulls feed on grasshoppers. In spite of its name, the California Gull is the state bird of Utah; it is recognized because a voracious flock of gulls saved the crops of settlers from an outbreak of ravenous grasshoppers in 1848.

Similar Species: Heermann's Gull (p. 69) is uniformly slate-gray and has a red bill and black legs. Ring-billed Gull (p. 70) has light eyes and a ring around its bill. Western Gull (p. 72) and Herring Gull are larger and have light eyes. Glaucous-winged Gull is larger and has light gray wing tips. Mew Gull is much smaller. Thayer's Gull has dark pink feet.

breeding

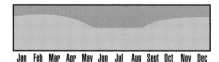

Jan Feb Mar Apr May Jun Jul Aug Sept Oct Nov Dec

Quick I.D.: mid-sized gull; white head and body; gray wings; black wing tips; greenish-yellow legs; dark eyes; sexes similar.
Size: 18–20 in.

Western Gull
Larus occidentalis

This abundant resident of the southern Pacific Coast is known to all area residents. These large, dark-backed gulls are easily encountered on a daily basis, and they are routinely seen soaring overhead or standing along a shoreline. The thousands of Western Gulls that live in San Diego help keep seashores, parking lots and city parks free of decaying organic matter.

Western Gulls are the only gulls to nest in southern California, and the Channel Islands host thousands of pairs annually. Many other seabirds also nest on these islands, which in turn provides Western Gulls with a seasonal bounty of eggs and young. Although these gulls prey on the nests and young of many seabirds, the colonies of these other species still survive and flourish.

Similar Species: Glaucous-winged Gull has a light gray back and wing covers, black eyes and gray wing tips. Mew Gull is much smaller and has black eyes and an all-yellow bill. Heermann's Gull (p. 69) is darker and has a red bill. California Gull (p. 71) is smaller and has yellow legs. Herring Gull (winter resident) has a lighter back and wing covers.

breeding

Quick I.D.: large gull; dark gray back and wing covers; white head; black wing tips; pink legs; yellow bill; yellow eyes; sexes similar. *Juvenile:* mottled brown overall.
Size: 24–26 in.

Jan Feb Mar Apr May Jun Jul Aug Sept Oct Nov Dec

Caspian Tern

Sterna caspia

breeding

Perhaps no other bird possesses such an odd North American breeding distribution as the Caspian Tern. Isolated colonies of Caspian Terns breed in pockets in Utah, in Wyoming, in British Columbia, in the Northwest Territories, near the Great Lakes, in Newfoundland and on the Pacific Coast of the United States. In the San Diego area, Caspian Terns nest in disturbed or human-created habitats, such as dikes and shorelines.

The Caspian Tern is the largest tern in North America, and it can be confused in flight only with gulls. Although it is the size of some of the area's smaller gulls, the Caspian Tern is easily identified by its lazy, stiff flight and its coral red bill. The species never reaches the abundance of many other gulls and terns in the area, but its formidable size results in a second look each spring from birders who have grown accustomed throughout winter to the smaller Forster's Tern.

Similar Species: Elegant Tern (p. 74) has a thin orange bill and a black crest. Forster's Tern (p. 75) and Common Tern are both much smaller and lack the heavy, red bill. Western Gull (p. 72) lacks the red bill and the black cap.

Quick I.D.: gull-sized; black cap; heavy, blood-red bill; light gray wing covers; white underparts; black legs; sexes similar.
In flight: shallowly forked tail; long, pointed wings; head pointed downward.
Size: 19–22½ in.

Jan Feb Mar Apr May Jun Jul Aug Sept Oct Nov Dec

Elegant Tern
Sterna elegans

non-breeding

Every day throughout the breeding season is a bad hair day for the Elegant Tern. Its ragged crest remains untamed, giving this fairly common bird a rebellious look. Looks are deceiving, however, because the Elegant Tern is one of our most loyal and charitable birds. Pairs arrive separately at their breeding sites and call out to one another in the hopes of recognizing their mate by voice. Once reunited, the male presents the female with what must be a tern's equivalent to a bouquet of roses and a box of chocolates: anchovies. Once the young have fledged, the pair may split off in their wanderings, possibly not encountering one another until the following April.

Until recently, Elegant Terns had not nested in southern California for years. In 1986, however, they returned to breed at a few protected beaches. The post-breeding wanderings of these birds, and those from colonies in Mexico, can be witnessed from July to October at San Diego Bay and San Elijo Lagoon. These acrobatic birds can be seen diving headfirst for anchovies and other small fish or posing regally aside other terns and gulls. The numbers of these birds seem to be steadily rising, and major population pulses appear to coincide with El Niño years.

Similar Species: Caspian Tern (p. 73) has a heavy red bill and lacks the shaggy crest. Forster's Tern (p. 75) lacks the shaggy crest and is smaller. Least Tern (p. 76) is much smaller and has a white forehead.

Quick I.D.: smaller than a gull; solid black cap with a shaggy crest; slender orange-yellow bill; dark legs; sexes similar.
Size: 16–17 in.

Jan Feb Mar Apr May Jun Jul Aug Sept Oct Nov Dec

Forster's Tern

Sterna forsteri

Wheeling about in mid-air to a stationary hover, the Forster's Tern carefully measures up its task before diving quickly into the water. The headfirst dive is often rewarded with the catch of a small fish, which is carried away in the bird's thin bill. The Forster's Tern breeds and winters in the San Diego area, and it can routinely be seen in foraging flights 30 to 60 feet above calm waters.

Terns fly effortlessly, bouncing lazily up and down in the rhythm of their wing beats. They superficially resemble gulls in body form, but their behavior differs dramatically. Terns rarely soar in the air, and they are infrequently seen resting on the water. While flying, terns usually have their bills pointed toward the water, and their forked tails are usually visible.

Similar Species: Caspian Tern (p. 73) is much larger and has an all-red bill. Common Tern has a darker red bill and legs, a mostly white tail and dark-tipped primaries. Elegant Tern (p. 74) is larger and has a longer, orange bill and a black crest. Least Tern (p. 76) is much smaller and has a white forehead.

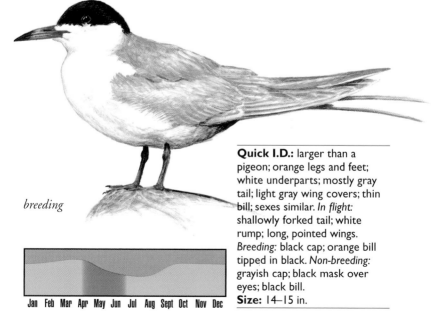

breeding

Jan Feb Mar Apr May Jun Jul Aug Sept Oct Nov Dec

Quick I.D.: larger than a pigeon; orange legs and feet; white underparts; mostly gray tail; light gray wing covers; thin bill; sexes similar. *In flight:* shallowly forked tail; white rump; long, pointed wings. *Breeding:* black cap; orange bill tipped in black. *Non-breeding:* grayish cap; black mask over eyes; black bill.
Size: 14–15 in.

Least Tern
Sterna antillarum

On long weekends during summer, one can appreciate the Least Tern's dilemma. Everyone crowds the beaches, so finding a place to call your own and lay down your towel is extremely difficult. Although humans visit southern California's beaches for pleasure, Least Terns are there out of necessity: they nest exclusively on open, sandy beaches. This tern's nest is a simple, hollow scrape in the sand where it lays and incubates one to three eggs. Provided that the nest is not raided by a predator or inadvertently destroyed by beach-goers, the young will hatch in 20 to 25 days.

Now restricted to a few scattered but protected breeding areas, such as McGrath State Park, North America's smallest tern is endangered. At these areas it is often possible to safely observe the Least Tern from a distance. Their courtship rituals are quite elaborate and include pre-nuptial flights and feeding interactions. Terns are among the few animals (including humans) that present gifts to potential mates. With an increase in our awareness, it is possible that both humans and species like the Least Tern can share the rich asset of southern California's beaches.

Similar Species: Forster's Tern (p. 75) and Common Tern are much larger, lack the white forehead and have red or orange bills.

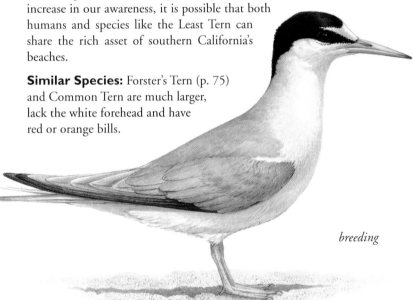

breeding

Quick I.D.: robin-sized; black cap; white forehead; yellow bill with a black tip; sexes similar. *In flight:* long, tapered wings with black outer edges.
Size: 9–10 in.

Jan Feb Mar Apr May Jun Jul Aug Sept Oct Nov Dec

Black Skimmer
Rynchops niger

breeding

There are many odd sights in southern California, but for the first-time birdwatcher the sight of a Black Skimmer must rank near the top of the list. This bird appears completely out of proportion: its lower mandible extends well beyond its upper one. Such a cumbersome bill looks wonderfully ridiculous, but when the skimmer's foraging strategy is known, the structure is justified.

With slow, deliberate wing beats, the Black Skimmer skims (what else would it do?) over calm waters. It flies so low that if it arches its neck down and holds its bill open, the lower mandible cuts through the water's surface. With the mandible now slicing through the water, small fish and invertebrates near the surface are seized with a lightning reflex.

For many years, Californians had no opportunity of observing this great adaptation. It wasn't until 1962 that California's first Black Skimmer was recorded, followed with breeding evidence in 1972. Now, birders from San Diego can be treated routinely to the unusual sights of Black Skimmers.

Similar Species: Caspian Tern (p. 73) has lighter upperparts and a shorter lower mandible.

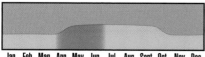

Jan Feb Mar Apr May Jun Jul Aug Sept Oct Nov Dec

Quick I.D.: smaller than a gull; red bill, tipped with black; lower mandible longer than upper; dark upperparts; light underparts; red legs; sexes similar.
Size: 16–20 in.

Rock Dove

Columba livia

The Rock Dove (or Pigeon) is the ruling king (or queen) of the urban canyon. It has taken to nesting and roosting on our skyscrapers, bridges and other buildings more readily than any other bird species. This Eurasian native, initially imported into North America as a food source, has turned the tables on humans: it routinely feasts on our handouts and leftovers.

Rock Doves may appear strained when walking—their heads moving back and forth with every step—but few birds are as agile in flight, or as abundant in urban and industrial areas. While no other bird varies as much in coloration, all Rock Doves, whether white, red, blue or mixed-pigment, will clap their wings above and below their bodies upon take-off.

Similar Species: Band-tailed Pigeon (p. 79) is larger, has a grayish tail band and lacks the white rump. Mourning Dove (p. 80) is the same length as a Rock Dove, but it is slender and has a long, tapering tail and olive-brown plumage.

Quick I.D.: mid-sized pigeon; variable color (iridescent blue-gray, black, red or white); white rump (usually); orange feet; fleshy base to bill; sexes similar.
Size: 13–14 in.

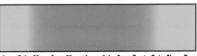

Jan Feb Mar Apr May Jun Jul Aug Sept Oct Nov Dec

Band-tailed Pigeon
Columba fasciata

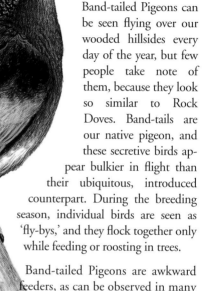

Band-tailed Pigeons can be seen flying over our wooded hillsides every day of the year, but few people take note of them, because they look so similar to Rock Doves. Band-tails are our native pigeon, and these secretive birds appear bulkier in flight than their ubiquitous, introduced counterpart. During the breeding season, individual birds are seen as 'fly-bys,' and they flock together only while feeding or roosting in trees.

Band-tailed Pigeons are awkward feeders, as can be observed in many of our forested city parks and golf courses. The birds cling clumsily to branches that bend under their weight. As the pigeons yo-yo up and down, they carefully pluck at the fruits of the Pacific madrone, which they find particularly appealing. Band-tails also visit backyard feeders in the early morning hours, usually cleaning them out before the homeowner awakes. Band-tailed Pigeons build their well-concealed nests among the upper branches of Douglas-fir, redwood and other trees.

Similar Species: Rock Dove (p. 78) is slightly smaller, has orange legs and usually has a white rump and white underwings.

Jan Feb Mar Apr May Jun Jul Aug Sept Oct Nov Dec

Quick I.D.: large pigeon; purple head and breast; white band at back of neck; grayish band on tail; gray rump; yellow bill tipped with black; dark underwings; sexes similar.
Size: 14–15½ in.

Mourning Dove
Zenaida macroura

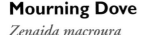

As a Mourning Dove bursts into flight, its wings 'clap' above and below its body for the first few wing beats. This dove is a swift, direct flier, and its wings can be heard whistling through the air. When the Mourning Dove is not in flight, its peaceful *cooooo-cooooo-cooooah* call can be heard filtering through open woodlands. These year-round residents roost inconspicuously in trees, but their soft cooing often betrays their presence.

The Mourning Dove feeds primarily on the ground, picking up grain and grit in open areas. It builds a flat, loose stick nest that rests flimsily on branches and trunks. Mourning Doves are attentive parents and, like other members of the pigeon family, they feed 'milk' to their young. It isn't true milk—since birds lack mammary glands— but a fluid produced by glands in the bird's crop. The chicks insert their bills down the adult's throat to eat the thick liquid.

Similar Species: Rock Dove (p. 78) has a white rump, is stockier and has a shorter tail. Band-tailed Pigeon (p. 79) has a shorter tail, and its plumage tends to be darker gray.

Quick I.D.: larger than a jay; gray-brown plumage; long, white-trimmed, tapering tail; sleek body; dark, shinny patch below ear; orange feet; dark bill; peach-colored underparts; sexes similar.

Size: 11–13 in.

Jan Feb Mar Apr May Jun Jul Aug Sept Oct Nov Dec

Barn Owl
Tyto alba

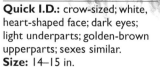

Barn Owls and humans have gradually entered into a mutually beneficial relationship. Before European colonization, Barn Owls nested primarily in snags, hollow trees and caves, hunting voles and mice in shrublands. With the arrival of Europeans and their rodent associates (house mice and black rats), however, the Barn Owl's diet underwent a slight shift. Barn Owls now commonly roost in old buildings and barns as well as in natural cavities, and they primarily hunt non-native rodents, much to the delight of present-day residents, who view the house mice and rats as agricultural and esthetic pests. Barn Owls have not been a complete benefactor of urbanization, because some die each year in collisions with cars and by injesting pesticides.

Similar Species: Great Horned Owl (p. 82) is darker gray and has ear tufts and yellow eyes.

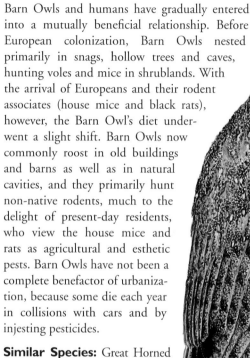

Jan	Feb	Mar	Apr	May	Jun	Jul	Aug	Sept	Oct	Nov	Dec

Quick I.D.: crow-sized; white, heart-shaped face; dark eyes; light underparts; golden-brown upperparts; sexes similar.
Size: 14–15 in.

Great Horned Owl
Bubo virginianus

The Great Horned Owl, the most widely distributed owl in North America, is among the most formidable of coastal predators. It uses specialized hearing, powerful talons and human-sized eyes during nocturnal hunts for mice, rabbits, quail, amphibians and occasionally fish. It has a poorly developed sense of smell, however, which is why it can prey on skunks—worn-out and discarded Great Horned Owl feathers are often identifiable by a simple sniff.

The deep, resonant hooting of the Great Horned Owl is easily imitated, often leading to interesting exchanges between bird and birder. The call's deep tone is not as distinctive as its pace, which closely follows the rhythm of *eat my food, I'll-eat yooou.*

Similar Species: Western Screech-Owl is much smaller and has vertical breast streaking. Long-eared Owl has a slimmer body and vertical breast streaking, and its ear tufts are very close together.

Quick I.D.: hawk-sized; large, widely spaced ear tufts; fine, horizontal breast bars; dark brown plumage; white throat; sexes similar.
Size: 18–25 in.

Jan   Feb   Mar   Apr   May   Jun   Jul   Aug   Sept   Oct   Nov   Dec

Lesser Nighthawk

Chordeiles acutipennis

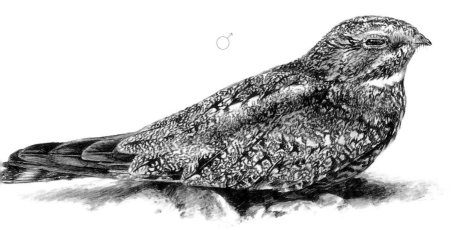

♂

Flying low over open fields at dusk, the Lesser Nighthawk feeds efficiently on flying insects. Appearing like a manic silhouette, the nighthawk zigzags across darkening skies in silence, wholly committed to foraging. Lesser Nighthawks belong to the goatsucker family, a most interesting group of birds that lead a double life. During the day, Lesser Nighthawks perch inconspicuously on the ground; at dusk, their flights are some of the night's ultimate activities. Aside from their quick, erratic flight, nighthawks are equipped with a very wide mouth gape fringed with feather shafts that effectively increase the size of the mouth for catching insects.

Lesser Nighthawks typically nest in southwestern deserts, but they do creep into our area by breeding on mesa tops, agricultural areas and desert scrub. They are very general in their choice of nesting sites, choosing any area of bare ground.

Similar Species: Common Poorwill has a shorter, rounded tail and wings, and the outer tail is tipped in white.

Jan Feb Mar Apr May Jun Jul Aug Sept Oct Nov Dec

Quick I.D.: smaller than a robin; mottled brown body; small bill; sexes similar.
In flight: long, pointed wings; pale bar across 'wrists'; white throat; long rectangular tail.
Size: 8–9 in.

Acorn Woodpecker

Melanerpes formicivorus

♂

In almost every sizable oak woodlot in our area, there lives a bird with habits that excite behavioral ecologists. The Acorn Woodpecker occurs over a relatively small geographic range, but its foraging and reproductive habits have given it worldwide recognition. These highly social woodpeckers remain in family units of up to a dozen related birds. Only a pair or two may actually breed; the remainder of the group helps the parents raise the young.

Communal breeding is very uncommon in birds, and it may be explained in the Acorn Woodpecker's case by its unusual food-hoarding behavior. The Acorn Woodpecker eats a wide variety of food items, from fruit to insects—the species name means 'ant eater'—and family groups store huge quantities of acorns (up to 20,000) in decaying trees. The family uses its acorn larder as an insurance policy against food shortages during winter. The larders require so much energy to collect and defend that it is possible only a sizable family group can effectively maintain one.

Similar Species: Other woodpeckers (pp. 85–86) lack the solid black back, white forehead and red cap.

Quick I.D.: smaller than a robin; black wings with white patches; white rump; black tail; white cheeks and forehead; black chin. *Male:* large red crown. *Female:* small red crown on back of head.
Size: 9 in.

Jan Feb Mar Apr May Jun Jul Aug Sept Oct Nov Dec

Nuttall's Woodpecker
Picoides nuttallii

The Nuttall's Woodpecker can often be seen hopping acrobatically on the undersides of branches and scaling up and down oak trunks. This woodpecker is almost entirely restricted to California, and is quite easily encountered in coastal woodlands. It seems to prefer dense, mature oak groves, hammering out nesting cavities in live or dead trees. Despite of its close association with oaks, the Nuttall's Woodpecker's diet is predominantly insectivorous, leaving the acorns to a neighboring family of Acorn Woodpeckers.

This energetic woodpecker was named for one of America's early naturalists, Thomas Nuttall. Nuttall was primarily a botanist, but he did pioneering work on many aspects of natural history all throughout America, including coastal California. Although another perfectly suitable name for this bird could have been the California Woodpecker, its accepted name honors one of the greatest natural scientists.

Similar Species: Acorn Woodpecker (p. 84) has an all-black back. Downy Woodpecker and Hairy Woodpecker lack the barring on their backs.

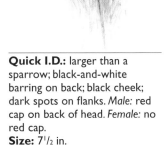

Jan	Feb	Mar	Apr	May	Jun	Jul	Aug	Sept	Oct	Nov	Dec

Quick I.D.: larger than a sparrow; black-and-white barring on back; black cheek; dark spots on flanks. *Male:* red cap on back of head. *Female:* no red cap.
Size: 7½ in.

Northern Flicker
Colaptes auratus

Walkers strolling through suburban neighborhoods may be surprised by a woodpecker flushing from the ground before them. As the Northern Flicker beats a hasty retreat, it reveals an unmistakable white rump and red wing linings. It is not as strictly arboreal as our other woodpeckers, and it spends more time feeding on the ground. Often, it is only when the Northern Flicker is around its nest cavity in a tree that it truly behaves like other woodpeckers: clinging, rattling and drumming.

The Northern Flicker can easily be seen all year, and it occasionally visits backyard feeders. This woodpecker (and other birds) squash ants and then preen themselves with the remains. Ants contain concentrations of formic acid, which is believed to kill small parasites living on the flicker's skin and in its feathers.

Similar Species: Other woodpeckers (pp. 84–85) and American Robin (p. 109) lack the white rump and red wing linings.

Quick I.D.: jay-sized; brown-barred back; spotted underparts; black bib; white rump; long bill. *Red-shafted* (main form in California): red wing and tail linings; brown crown. *Yellow-shafted* (rare in California in winter): yellow wing and tail linings; gray crown; red nape. *Male red-shafted:* red mustache. *Male yellow-shafted:* black mustache. *Female:* no mustache. **Size:** 11–14 in.

| Jan | Feb | Mar | Apr | May | Jun | Jul | Aug | Sept | Oct | Nov | Dec |

Anna's Hummingbird

Calypte anna

The male Anna's Hummingbird is the most distinctive hummingbird in southern California. Although residents meet many hummingbirds in their gardens and city parks, no other male 'hummer' has its head and neck draped in a similar rose red splendor that dances with the sun's rays: Anna's is the only hummingbird on the continent to show this feature.

The Anna's Hummingbird nests in backyard gardens, chaparral shrublands, oak woodlands and savannahs. Following its early spring nesting period, most birds undergo a post-breeding movement to the north and upslope to take advantage of late-blooming flowers. Once the cool winds of late summer begin to blow through the high country, most Anna's Hummingbirds in the San Diego area retreat to the lowlands for the remainder of the year.

Similar Species: Male is distinctive. Female Rufous Hummingbird (p. 88) and Allen's Hummingbird have rufous-brown flanks.

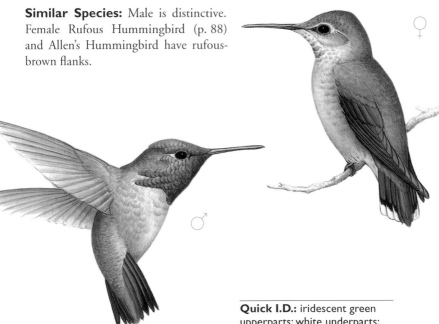

Jan Feb Mar Apr May Jun Jul Aug Sept Oct Nov Dec

Quick I.D.: iridescent green upperparts; white underparts; long, narrow bill. *Male:* rose throat and head; green band around waist. *Female:* green crown; rose-spotted throat; light green flanks.
Size: 3¹/₂–4¹/₂ in.

Rufous Hummingbird
Selasphorus rufus

The Rufous Hummingbird's gentle appearance is misleading: in spring, the male is fiercely aggressive and will chase intruders away in the spirited defense of a food source. Hummingbirds are easily attracted to backyard feeders filled with sweetened water (one part sugar: four parts water). They are also attracted to red objects, and have been known to closely investigate shirts, lanterns or other backyard objects that are bright red.

The tiny male performs his towering courtship flight with great speed, which makes it difficult to follow. Performing before a prospective mate, the male's noisy, buzzy flight follows an inverted 'U' pattern. The male climbs high, with his rusty back facing the female, and then from great heights turns and dives quickly toward the female with his crimson throat blazing.

Similar Species: Male Anna's Hummingbird (p. 87) has a rose head and throat, but is otherwise green and is larger.

Quick I.D.: much smaller than a sparrow. *Male:* orange-brown back, tail and flanks; scarlet, scaled throat; green crown. *Female:* green back; rufous sides; red spots on throat.
Size: 4 in.

Jan Feb Mar Apr May Jun Jul Aug Sept Oct Nov Dec

Pacific-slope Flycatcher
Empidonax difficilis

Fortunately for birders, the Pacific-slope Flycatcher's song is much more distinctive than its plumage. When you enter any moist woodland during spring, this flycatcher's snappy *pawee* is always one of the first sounds you'll hear. This common songbird, formerly grouped with the Cordilleran Flycatcher into a single species—the Western Flycatcher—arrives in San Diego in March and leaves before the end of September.

The genus name *Empidonax* means, quite appropriately, 'lord of the mosquitoes,' and this bird uses the foraging technique made famous by its family. From its perch on a shady limb, this small bird launches after a flying insect, seizes it in mid-air and loops back to alight on the same perch it vacated.

Similar Species: Willow Flycatcher (uncommon migrant) has a very faint eye ring, and its song is *fitz-bew*. Olive-sided Flycatcher has a dark vest, and its song is *quick-three-beers*. Western Wood-Pewee has no eye ring and is dusky-colored.

Jan Feb Mar Apr May Jun Jul Aug Sept Oct Nov Dec

Quick I.D.: sparrow-sized; olive-green upperparts; yellow-green underparts; white eye ring; two wing bars; dark bill; yellow wash on belly; dark wings and tail; sexes similar.
Size: 5–6 in.

Black Phoebe
Sayornis nigricans

The Black Phoebe often flycatches from a low perch, and then, unlike many flycatchers, it alights on a different perch after seizing an insect. Often, Black Phoebes can be watched wagging their tails from a fencetop perch in your backyard.

Some Black Phoebes are present year-round, while others are migratory. They usually build their mud-and-grass nests under a bridge, culvert, picnic shelter or eave to gain refuge from the California rains. Because the Black Phoebe constructs its small cup nest one mouthful at a time, it often selects a site near a mud puddle to save on valuable construction time.

Similar Species: Other flycatchers tend to be olive-green or brown. Dark-eyed Junco (p. 131) has a rusty back and flanks and a conical bill, and it feeds mainly on the ground.

Quick I.D.: sparrow-sized; black upperparts, tail and breast; white belly and undertail coverts; sexes similar.
Size: 6¹/₂–7¹/₂ in.

Jan Feb Mar Apr May Jun Jul Aug Sept Oct Nov Dec

Western Kingbird

Tyrannus verticalis

The tumble-flight courtship display of the Western Kingbird is one of the most entertaining spring scenes in southern California. While twisting and turning, the male flies 60 feet straight up, then suddenly stalls, tumbles, flips and twists as he falls toward the ground. Western Kingbirds perform this spectacle each spring over undeveloped, open grasslands throughout our area. Once pair bonds are formed, the nest is built on a ledge or utility pole, or atop an abandoned nest, where the female lays three to five eggs.

For much of their time in southern California, Western Kingbirds are commonly seen perched on fenceposts, barbed wire and power lines, surveying for prey. Once prey is sighted, kingbirds may persistently chase the flying insects for up to 40 feet before the bird snaps its bill upon its meal.

Similar Species: Cassin's Kingbird has a darker head and throat and no white outer tail feathers.

Quick I.D.: smaller than a robin; yellow belly; light gray head and throat; dark wings and tail; white outer tail feathers; sexes similar.
Size: 8–9 in.

White-throated Swift
Aeronautes saxatalis

The White-throated Swift is one of the frequent fliers of the bird world; only incubation keeps this bird off its wings. It feeds, drinks, bathes and even mates in flight. During its 10- to 11-year average lifespan, these sailors of the air may travel more than one million miles.

The White-throated Swift is a year-round resident of the San Diego area, and it can be encountered on a daily basis throughout summer. These high-flying aeronauts often forage for flying insects at great heights, and they are often visible only as sky specks. This swift nests on vertical crevices, which in our area includes cliffs, horizontal cracks, headlands, buildings and overpasses.

Similar Species: Vaux's Swift and Black Swift lack the contrasting white and dark underparts. Northern Rough-winged Swallow and Bank Swallow lack the dark flanks and the wing pits.

Quick I.D.: black upperparts; white throat tapering to belly; black flanks; slender, sleek body; very small legs; sexes similar.
In flight: long, tapering wings that angle back; long, shallowly forked tail.
Size: 6¹/₂–7 in.

Jan Feb Mar Apr May Jun Jul Aug Sept Oct Nov Dec

Tree Swallow

Tachycineta bicolor

Depending on food availability, Tree Swallows may forage over great distances, darting above open fields and wetlands as they catch flying insects in their bills. These bicolored birds occasionally sweep down to the water surface for a quick drink and bath. In bad weather, Tree Swallows may fly up to five miles to distant marshes or lakes to find flying insects.

The Tree Swallow is among the first migrants to arrive in the San Diego area. It returns to our freshwater marshes in late January, often beating the onset of spring weather. Most of the Tree Swallows we see continue on to northern California to nest; this species is a very local summer resident in southern California.

Similar Species: Violet-green Swallow (p. 94) has a white cheek and a white rump patch. Northern Rough-winged Swallow and Bank Swallow lack the green upperparts.

Quick I.D.: sparrow-sized; iridescent blue-green plumage; white underparts; no white on cheek; dark rump; small bill; long, pointed wings; shallowly forked tail; small feet; sexes similar.

Size: 5–6 in.

Jan Feb Mar Apr May Jun Jul Aug Sept Oct Nov Dec

Violet-green Swallow

Tachycineta thalassina

One of the first swallows to return to our area in spring, the Violet-green Swallow soars, dips and dives in forest clearings, fields, marshes and around buildings. These natural flyers spend much of their lives on the wing, and they are frequently seen in the company of look-alike Tree Swallows. It is in these mixed flocks that the Violet-green Swallows' white cheeks and 'saddle patches' distinguish them from their peers.

Few Violet-green Swallows nest in the San Diego area; most move to woodlands in the foothills and mountains, where they nest in old wood-pecker holes and natural cavities in trees and cliffs.

Similar Species: Tree Swallow (p. 93) lacks the white face and white saddle patches. Most other swallows lack the dark green back and white underparts.

Quick I.D.: sparrow-sized; iridescent green above; white below; white face and 'saddle patches'; short tail; sexes similar.
Size: 5–6 in.

Jan Feb Mar Apr May Jun Jul Aug Sept Oct Nov Dec

Cliff Swallow

Petrochelidon pyrrhonota

The Cliff Swallow is our most widespread swallow, and you can often encounter it by the hundreds. Cliff Swallows nest under many of the bridges that span our waters, and clouds of them will sometimes whip up on either side of a bridge. They do not restrict their nesting to bridges, however, and colonies are occasionally found under piers, on vacated structures and on dry, rocky cliffs.

If you stop to inspect the undersides of a bridge, you may see hundreds of gourd-shaped nests stuck to the pillars and structural beams. The nests are meticulously made from mud, one mouthful at a time. As they busily build their nests, hundreds of Cliff Swallows create a chaotic scene with their constant procession back and forth between nest and mudflat.

Similar Species: Tree Swallow (p. 93) has a blue-green back. Barn Swallow has a deeply forked tail and a dark rump. Northern Rough-winged Swallow and Vaux's Swift lack the light rump and forehead and the rusty cheeks.

Jan Feb Mar Apr May Jun Jul Aug Sept Oct Nov Dec

Quick I.D.: sparrow-sized; pale forehead; buff rump; dark back with white stripes; gray-brown wings and tail; white underparts; rusty cheeks; dark bib; square tail; sexes similar.

Size: 5–6 in.

Western Scrub-Jay

Aphelocoma californica

The Western Scrub-Jay is a bird of open forests, especially scrub and chaparral where it can be seen perched high, evaluating its territory. While walking through chaparral, open woodlands and residential areas, you may see (and hear) the scrub-jay busily foraging. It frequently buries acorns by pounding them into soft soil and covering them with leaf litter or small stones. Many of the acorns are never retrieved, making scrub-jays effective dispersers for oak trees.

This bird is one of the few species that is able to eat hairy caterpillars. A caterpillar's guard hairs are an effective defense mechanism because they irritate the digestive tracts of most birds. Western Scrub-Jays, however, have overcome this defense: they rub down the caterpillars in sand or soil before eating them, effectively 'shaving off' the irritating hairs. Scrub-jays have a varied diet, also eating spiders, beetles, wasps, termites, nuts, corn, fruit, lizards and small rodents, and they visit feeders stocked with sunflower seeds, suet and peanuts.

Similar Species: Steller's Jay has a crest, a dark blue body and a black hood.

Quick I.D.: larger than a robin; blue head, back and tail; white throat; gray belly; long tail; no crest; sexes similar.
Size: 11–13 in.

Jan Feb Mar Apr May Jun Jul Aug Sept Oct Nov Dec

American Crow
Corvus brachyrhynchos

The American Crow calls with the classic, long, descending *caaaw*. In late summer and fall, when their reproductive duties are completed, crows group together to roost in flocks, known as a 'murders.' For unknown reasons, the crow population has exploded in our area in recent years, and large flocks can be seen almost anywhere.

This large, black bird's intelligence has led it into many confrontations with human's, from which it often emerges the victor. Scientific studies have shown that crows can solve simple problems, which comes as no surprise to anyone who has watched crows drop shellfish from the air onto rocks, cracking the shells and exposing the meaty flesh.

Similar Species: Common Raven (p. 98) is much larger and has a diamond-shaped tail.

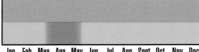

Jan Feb Mar Apr May Jun Jul Aug Sept Oct Nov Dec

Quick I.D.: small gull–sized; black; fan-shaped tail; slim overall; sexes similar.
Size: 18–20 in.

Common Raven

Corvus corax

Common Ravens are often seen gliding effortlessly on updrafts over the city and into the mountains and deserts, offering their hoarse voices to the misty air. Whether stealing food from a flock of gulls, harassing an eagle in mid-air, or confidently strutting among campers at a favorite park, the raven is worthy of its reputation as a clever bird. Glorified in traditional cultures worldwide, ravens are not restricted to the instinctive behaviors of most other birds. With the ability to express themselves playfully—tumbling aimlessly through the air or teaming up against a coyote—these large, raucous birds flaunt traits many think of as exclusively human.

Similar Species: American Crow (p. 97) is much smaller and has a fan-shaped tail. Hawks (pp. 47–49) have fan-shaped tails and are not completely black.

Quick I.D.: larger than a hawk; black; large bill; spade-shaped tail; shaggy throat; sexes similar. *In flight:* spreads primaries.
Size: 22–24 in.

Jan Feb Mar Apr May Jun Jul Aug Sept Oct Nov Dec

Oak Titmouse
Baeolophus inornatus

The nasal *tsick-a-der-der* call of the Oak Titmouse is a sound of mature mixed-oak forests. These little birds are ordinary-looking, but an oak wood would seem empty without their subtle presence. The Oak Titmouse nests in natural cavities, rotted-out stumps and occasionally in abandoned woodpecker nests. It may even partially excavate a cavity in a soft decaying tree. It lines its nesting cavity with fur, moss and other soft materials.

The Oak Titmouse frequently pairs up with the same mate throughout its short life, which seldom exceeds five years. The name 'titmouse' comes from European sources: *tit* is Scandinavian for 'little,' and 'mouse' is a corruption of *mase*, the Old English word for 'bird.'

Similar Species: Bushtit (p. 100) is smaller and has a relatively longer tail. Hutton's Vireo has white wing bars and a faint eye ring, and it does not have a crest.

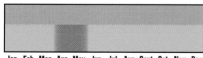

Jan Feb Mar Apr May Jun Jul Aug Sept Oct Nov Dec

Quick I.D.: sparrow-sized; gray-brown back, tail and wings; small crest; gray underparts; sexes similar.
Size: 5 1/2 in.

Bushtit
Psaltriparus minimus

The character of the home reflects the quality of the occupant, and the tiny, gray Bushtit sets a fine example. The architecture of its nest is worth a close look: the intricate weaving of fine fibers, spiderwebs, grasses, mosses and lichens results in what you might mistake for an old gray sock hanging from a brushy shrub.

Their gray-brown bodies are nondescript, but Bushtits are easy to identify because of their foraging behavior: they tend to hang in every position possible while they feed. Surprisingly tiny, these tufts of continually moving feathers travel in loose flocks, appearing from dense tangles and bushes in all corners of the city. During winter, they frequently visit backyard feeding stations, and they are very fond of suet. Bushtits often boldly approach close enough to make binoculars unnecessary.

Similar Species: Oak Titmouse (p. 99) has a small crest and a relatively shorter tail.

Quick I.D.: larger than a hummingbird; light brown cap; dusty gray overall; long tail; sexes similar.
Size: 3–4 in.

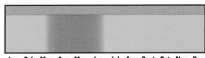

Jan Feb Mar Apr May Jun Jul Aug Sept Oct Nov Dec

Wrentit

Chamaea fasciata

For every Wrentit they see, San Diego residents can expect to hear dozens more. This small, secretive songbird's voice permeates dense chaparral and coastal scrub communities throughout our area. The distinctive, bouncy song accelerates like a ping pong ball coming to rest.

Typical Wrentit habitat consists of a nearly continuous layer of brush, with no more than a few yards of gap for the small birds to cross. These long-tailed, year-round residents breed exclusively in the Pacific Coast states. They usually build their nests about two feet off the ground in coastal sage and coyote brush thickets, carefully concealing them from nest-robbing Western Scrub-Jays.

Similar Species: Oak Titmouse (p. 99) has a small crest, dark eyes and a relatively shorter tail. Bushtit (p. 100) is smaller and has gray, unstreaked plumage. Bewick's Wren (p. 103) has white eyebrows and light underparts. Winter Wren has a much shorter tail.

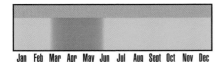

Jan Feb Mar Apr May Jun Jul Aug Sept Oct Nov Dec

Quick I.D.: sparrow-sized; grayish-brown plumage; long, rounded tail (often cocked up); fine breast streaks; small, dark bill; yellow eyes; sexes similar.
Size: 6–6¹/₂ in.

Pygmy Nuthatch
Sitta pygmaea

The Pygmy Nuthatch is one of the most energetic residents of yellow pine forests: it hops continuously up and down trunks and treetops, incessantly probing and calling its high-pitched *te-dee te-dee*. Unlike other birds that forage on tree trunks, nuthatches routinely work their way down trees headfirst. Because of their unusual approach, nuthatches are able to find seeds and invertebrates that woodpeckers and creepers missed.

The Pygmy Nuthatch is quite gregarious, and it often appears in small flocks that increase in size during fall and winter. On winter nights, Pygmy Nuthatches retreat to communal roosts in cavities where many birds can snuggle together.

Similar Species: White-breasted Nuthatch is larger and has a black crown and reddish or rusty undertail coverts. Red-breasted Nuthatch has a black eye line and reddish underparts.

Quick I.D.: smaller than a sparrow; brownish cap bordered by dark eye line; white cheek and throat; gray-blue back; short tail; buff-colored underparts; straight bill; sexes similar.
Size: 4–4¹/₂ in.

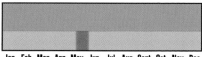

Jan Feb Mar Apr May Jun Jul Aug Sept Oct Nov Dec

Bewick's Wren

Thryomanes bewickii

The Bewick's Wren ranges throughout California. It is the most common wren in our area, especially in shrubby habitats: it prefers the undergrowth of our parks and the ornamental shrubs in our yards. These year-round singers are always more abundant than they seem to be, and they frequently nest in backyard nest boxes, natural cavities, wood piles, sheds and garages.

The mission in this wren's life appears to involve the investigation of all suspicious noises, which makes it an easy bird to attract. Their easily identifiable songs seem individualized, as though each male has added his own twist. Learning the tone and quality of the Bewick's Wren's song is the best way to find this bird.

Similar Species: Winter Wren and House Wren both lack the white eyebrow and have shorter tails. Marsh Wren (p. 104) has a streaked back and lives in marshes.

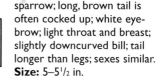

Jan Feb Mar Apr May Jun Jul Aug Sept Oct Nov Dec

Quick I.D.: smaller than a sparrow; long, brown tail is often cocked up; white eyebrow; light throat and breast; slightly downcurved bill; tail longer than legs; sexes similar.
Size: 5–5 1/2 in.

Marsh Wren

Cistothorus palustris

This energetic little bird usually lives in cattail marshes and dense, wet meadows bordered by willows. Although it usually sings deep in the vegetation, its distinctive voice is one of the characteristic sounds of our freshwater wetlands. In early spring, many wetlands ring with the dynamic call of this reclusive bird. The song has the repetitive quality of an old sewing machine, and once you learn the rhythm, you will hear it whenever you visit freshwater wetlands. The Marsh Wren was formerly a more widespread breeder, but its populations are steadily declining.

A typical sighting of a Marsh Wren is spotting a brown blur moving noisily about within shoreline tangles. Although the wren may be less than three yards from the observer, its cryptic habits and appearance are effective camouflage. Patient observers may be rewarded with a brief glimpse of a Marsh Wren perching high atop a cattail reed as it quickly evaluates its territory.

Similar Species: Bewick's (p. 103), Winter and House wrens all have unstreaked backs and generally avoid wetlands.

Quick I.D.: smaller than a sparrow; brown overall; white streaking on back; white eye line; light throat and breast; cocked-up tail; sexes similar.
Size: 4–5¹⁄₂ in.

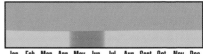

Jan Feb Mar Apr May Jun Jul Aug Sept Oct Nov Dec

Ruby-crowned Kinglet
Regulus calendula

Ruby-crowned Kinglets are common winter visitors to San Diego's parks and backyards, especially among coniferous trees. They arrive in September and flit continuously through our shrubs until May. Kinglets always appear nervous, with their tails and wings flicking continuously as they hop from branch to branch in search of grubs and insect eggs.

The Ruby-crowned Kinglet is similar to the Golden-crowned Kinglet in size, habits and coloration, but it has a hidden ruby crown. 'Rubies' are heard more often then they are seen, especially prior to their spring departure (February to April). Their distinctive song starts like a motor chugging to life, and then the kinglets fire off a series of loud, rising *chewy-chewy-chewy-chewys*. These final phrases are often the only recognizable part of the song.

Similar Species: Golden-crowned Kinglet has a black outline to the crown. Hutton's Vireo is larger and stouter and has a stubby bill. Orange-crowned Warbler (p. 111) has no wing bars.

Quick I.D.: smaller than a sparrow; plump; dark olive; white wing bars; dark tail and wings; incomplete eye ring. *Male:* red crown (infrequently seen). *Female:* no red crown.
Size: 4 in.

Jan Feb Mar Apr May Jun Jul Aug Sept Oct Nov Dec

Blue-gray Gnatcatcher
Polioptila caerulea

♂

breeding

The Blue-gray Gnatcatcher's tail is almost as long as its body, and it constantly waves its tail lazily during its tree-top foraging. Even in soft winds, the gnatcatcher's tail catches the breeze, and appears to nearly topple the small bird. Gnatcatchers are energetic birds that flit out to catch flying insects or bounce along branches looking for prey. Although these bird undoubtedly eat gnats, those insects do not represent a substantial portion of their diet.

Coastal sage scrub in our area is the last remaining habitat for the endangered California Gnatcatcher. It is far more frequently encountered in news headlines than in the wild, because many of its last vestiges of habitat are being threatened by development. The few remaining areas in San Diego to observe this endangered species include San Elijo Lagoon Sanctuary and Border Field State Park.

Similar Species: California Gnatcatcher has an all-black tail with tiny white spots on the underneath. Ruby-crowned Kinglet (p. 105) and Golden-crowned Kinglet are olive-green overall and have short tails and wing bars. Gray Catbird is much larger and has red undertail coverts.

Quick I.D.: smaller than a sparrow; blue-gray upperparts; long tail; white eye ring; pale gray underparts; no wing bars; tail is black above with white outer tail feathers. *Breeding male:* dark blue-gray upperparts; black-bordered crown. *Female:* light gray upperparts.
Size: 4½–5 in.

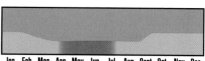

Jan Feb Mar Apr May Jun Jul Aug Sept Oct Nov Dec

Western Bluebird

Sialia mexicana

Dressed with the colors of a clear summer sky on its back and the warm setting sun on its breast, the male Western Bluebird looks like a little piece of pure sky come to life. To fully appreciate this open-country specialty, try to spot a male on a crisp, clear spring morning.

The Western Bluebird breeds in open oak woodlands and open coniferous forests. Unfortunately, it has lost many of its nesting sites in natural cavities to House Sparrows and European Starlings, and to the removal of dead trees from California's agricultural areas.

Similar Species: Male Lazuli Bunting (p. 141) is smaller and has a conical bill.

Quick I.D.: smaller than a robin; white undertail coverts; thin bill. *Male:* deep blue upperparts and throat; rufous-brown breast and flanks. *Female:* duller, brownish-gray head and back; duller blue wings and tail; lighter chestnut breast and flanks.
Size: 6$\frac{1}{2}$–7 in.

Jan Feb Mar Apr May Jun Jul Aug Sept Oct Nov Dec

Hermit Thrush

Catharus guttatus

The Hermit Thrush is a common winter visitor in lowland brushy areas and woodlands. Large numbers of this thrush winter in southern California, but because it is a shy species, it is not readily observed. Hermit Thrushes are, however, attracted to birdbaths.

It is unfortunate that the Hermit Thrush does not nest in San Diego—it moves north and into the mountains for its breeding duties—because it is an inspired songster. Its enchanting song can be heard in the mountains early on spring mornings, and it is routinely the last of the daytime singers to be silenced by night.

Similar Species: Swainson's Thrush has a prominent, buff eye ring, golden-brown cheeks and a rusty-brown back. Young American Robin (p. 109) lacks the uniformly brown back. Fox Sparrow (p. 128) has a conical bill.

Quick I.D.: smaller than a robin; pale white eye ring; reddish rump and tail; lightly spotted throat and breast; white belly and undertail coverts; gray flanks; sexes similar.
Size: 5–7¹/₂ in.

Jan Feb Mar Apr May Jun Jul Aug Sept Oct Nov Dec

American Robin
Turdus migratorius

If not for its abundance, the American Robin's voice and plumage would inspire pause and praise from casual onlookers. However, acclimatization has dealt the robin an unfair hand, and it is generally not fully appreciated for the pleasures it offers the eyes and ears of San Diego residents.

Nevertheless, the American Robin's close relationship with urban areas has allowed many residents an insight into a bird's life. A robin dashing around a yard in search of worms or ripe berries is as familiar to many people as its three-part *cheerily-cheery up-cheerio* song. Robins also make up part of the emotional landscape of communities as their cheery song, their spotted young and occasionally even their deaths are experiences shared by their human neighbors.

American Robins appear to be year-round residents in San Diego, but it is possible that the bird dashing on your lawn in June is not the same bird as the one you see in February. Unnoticed by most residents, the neighborhood robins take seasonal shifts; new birds arrive from the north and east when some summer residents depart for southern climes in fall.

Similar Species: Immature robins can be confused with other thrushes, but robins always have at least a hint of red in the breast.

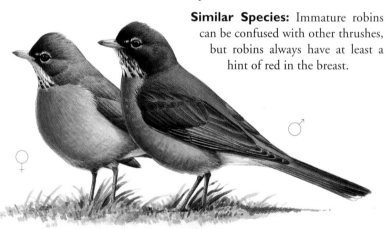

Jan Feb Mar Apr May Jun Jul Aug Sept Oct Nov Dec

Quick I.D.: smaller than a jay; dark head, back and tail; yellow bill; striped throat; white under-tail coverts. *Male:* brick-red breast; darker hood. *Female:* slightly more orange breast; lighter hood.
Size: 9–11 in.

Warbling Vireo
Vireo gilvus

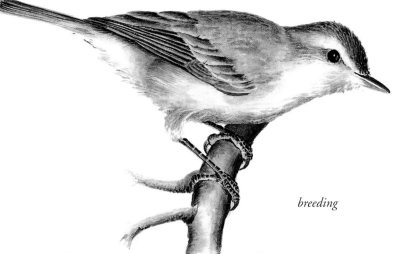

breeding

The Warbling Vireo can be quite common during the summer months, but you still need to make a prolonged search before spotting this bird. Lacking any splashy field marks, the Warbling Vireo is exceedingly difficult to spot unless it moves. Searching the treetops for this inconspicuous bird may be a literal 'pain in the neck,' but the satisfaction in visually confirming its identity can be rewarding.

The velvety voice of the Warbling Vireo contrasts sharply with its dull, nondescript plumage. The often-repeated *I love you, I love you ma'am!* song delights the listening forest with its oscillating quality. The phrases finish on an upbeat, as if the bird is asking a question of the wilds.

Similar Species: Hutton's Vireo has two wing bars, is much smaller and has an incomplete eye ring. Oak Titmouse (p. 99) has a pointed crest and no eyebrow. Orange-crowned Warbler (p. 111) is smaller and has more olive-green upperparts and yellowish underparts.

Quick I.D.: smaller than a sparrow; white eyebrow; no wing bars; olive-gray upperparts; greenish flanks; light underparts; gray crown; sexes similar.
Size: 4¹/₂–5¹/₂ in.

Jan Feb Mar Apr May Jun Jul Aug Sept Oct Nov Dec

Orange-crowned Warbler
Vermivora celata

The Orange-crowned Warbler's fame lies not in any one outstanding feature; rather, it is this warbler's noticeable lack of distinguishing traits that sets it apart. In fact, the most obvious feature of this noble warbler is its complete lack of any distinctive field marks. The scientific name *celata* means 'to conceal in,' and it refers to this warbler's infrequently seen orange crown. It could just as easily refer to its unmarked dress. Fortunately for the easily frustrated birder, the bird's tinkling tones are distinctive, because the soft trill breaks down at the mid-point.

The Orange-crowned Warbler is common in the San Diego area throughout the year. It nests and feeds in shrubby thickets in city parks, undeveloped lands and occasionally in forested backyards, where bushes echo with their descending trill.

Similar Species: Yellow Warbler (p. 112), Wilson's Warbler (p. 116) and Hutton's Vireo all have distinctive field marks.

Jan Feb Mar Apr May Jun Jul Aug Sept Oct Nov Dec

Quick I.D.: smaller than a sparrow; dusky yellow underparts; darker upperparts; faint orange crown (rarely seen); sexes similar.
Size: 4–5 in.

Yellow Warbler
Dendroica petechia

The Yellow Warbler is common in shrublands and in groves of birch, willow and cottonwood. From mid-April through September, this brilliantly colored warbler is easily found in appropriate riparian habitats. During our winters, Yellow Warblers migrate to the tropics, spending September to April in Mexico and South America.

The Yellow Warbler's courtship song is a lively *sweet-sweet-sweet I'm so-so sweet.* Despite its eight-month absence, the Yellow Warbler is easily recognized in early May, because its song is so distinctive. In true warbler fashion, the summertime activities of the Yellow Warbler are energetic and inquisitive, flitting from branch to branch in search of juicy caterpillars, aphids and beetles.

Similar Species: Orange-crowned Warbler (p. 111) lacks the red breast streaks. Wilson's Warbler (p. 116) has a small black cap.

Quick I.D.: smaller than a sparrow; yellow overall; darker back, wings and tail; dark eyes and bill. *Male:* fine, red breast streaking. *Female:* no red streaking.
Size: 4–5 in.

Jan Feb Mar Apr May Jun Jul Aug Sept Oct Nov Dec

Yellow-rumped Warbler
Dendroica coronata

♀

♂

breeding

The Yellow-rumped Warbler is the Cadillac of birds: it has all the extras—wing bars, crown, breast streaks, colored rump, etc. In winter and during migrations, the Yellow-rumped Warbler is abundant throughout the San Diego area, often crowding into flowing eucalyptus; during summer this bird retreats to the mountains.

The western race of the Yellow-rumped Warbler has a glorious yellow throat. It was formerly called the Audubon's Warbler, distinguishing it from the white-throated eastern form, which was known as the Myrtle Warbler. Ironically, although the western race bore the name of one of the greatest ornithologists, it was one of the few birds that Audubon never met. Although it no longer officially holds the Audubon title, many western birders continue to refer to this spry bird by its former name, affirming its western roots.

Similar Species: Townsend's Warbler (p. 114) and Black-throated Gray Warbler both lack the combination of a yellow rump and whitish underparts. Eastern Yellow-rumped Warbler (Myrtle Warbler) has a white throat and occurs mostly in wetter habitats.

Quick I.D.: smaller than a sparrow; blue-black back, tail and wings; yellow rump, shoulder patches and crown; yellow throat; white wing bars; dark breast band; white belly; dark cheek. *Male:* bright colors. *Female:* less intense colors.
Size: 5–6 in.

Jan Feb Mar Apr May Jun Jul Aug Sept Oct Nov Dec

Townsend's Warbler
Dendroica townsendi

The Townsend's Warbler breeds in the coniferous forests of the Pacific Northwest, and it is a common transient through the San Diego area. It can usually be found in spring—from mid-April to mid-May—and again in fall—from late August into October.

During migration, Townsend's Warblers are usually found in mixed flocks with other warblers and vireos. They pass through a wide variety of lowland habitats in our area, including riparian and oak woodlands, suburban gardens and parks. The Townsend's Warblers' bold colors, flitting habits and unmistakable *weezy weezy weezy twee* songs help distinguish them from most other warblers.

Similar Species: Black-throated Gray Warbler lacks the yellow plumage. Hermit Warbler (with which it sometimes forms hybrids) lacks the black cheek patch.

Quick I.D.: smaller than a sparrow; black throat; yellow face; dark cheek patch; olive back; dark wings and tail; white wing bars. *Male:* larger black bib.
Size: 4¹/₂–5 in.

Jan Feb Mar Apr May Jun Jul Aug Sept Oct Nov Dec

Common Yellowthroat
Geothlypis trichas

With so much diversity within North America's wood warbler clan, it is no surprise that one species has forsaken forests in favor of cattail marshes. The male Common Yellowthroat is easily identified either by his black mask or by his oscillating *witchety-witchety-witchety* song. In our area, this energetic warbler reaches its highest abundance among wetland brambles and cattails, but it can be seen and heard in the vegetation bordering many freshwater bodies.

Female yellowthroats are rarely seen because they keep to their nests, deep within the thick vegetation surrounding marshes. The Common Yellowthroat's nests are often parasitized by the Brown-headed Cowbird. Should a pair avoid this common nest parasite, three to five young yellowthroats will hatch after only about 12 days of incubation. These young continue their rapid development; they soon leave the nest, allowing the parents to repeat the process once again.

Similar Species: Male is distinct. Female Nashville Warbler has dark brown legs.

Quick I.D.: smaller than a sparrow; orange legs; yellow throat and underparts; olive upperparts. *Male:* black mask with white border on forehead. *Female:* no mask.

Size: 4½–5½ in.

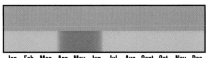

Jan Feb Mar Apr May Jun Jul Aug Sept Oct Nov Dec

Wilson's Warbler
Wilsonia pusilla

The hearty chatter of the Wilson's Warbler reveals the presence of this small, colorful bird. It feeds energetically on caterpillars and other insects in branches that are low to the ground, often near water. Often flitting to within a branch of onlookers, this energetic warbler bounces from one perch to another like an overwound wind-up toy.

This warbler was named for Alexander Wilson, the father of American ornithology. During its spring and fall migrations, the Wilson's Warbler can be found almost anywhere in San Diego, including well-planted backyards. During the summer, however, it is usually absent from San Diego, moving into the mountains to nest.

Similar Species: Orange-crowned Warbler (p. 111) has greener plumage and lacks the black cap. Yellow Warbler (p. 112) has a streaked breast and lacks the black cap.

Quick I.D.: smaller than a sparrow; lemon-yellow underparts; olive to dark green upperparts. *Male:* black cap. *Female:* duller cap.
Size: 4¹/₂–5 in.

Jan Feb Mar Apr May Jun Jul Aug Sept Oct Nov Dec

Western Tanager
Piranga ludoviciana

Arriving in San Diego woodlands in mid-April, the male Western Tanager, which is splashed with red, yellow and black, sings robin-like songs high in the forest canopy. This species is one of San Diego's most beautiful birds, and every possible encounter with it should be fully enjoyed.

Despite the male tanager's colorful attire, he often remains inconspicuous on his breeding grounds in local mountains. Tracing the easily learned song and *pit-a-tik* call to its source is the best way to discover this tropically dressed bird, which frequently remains on the same treetop perch for long periods of time.

Similar Species: Bullock's Oriole (p. 136) and Black-headed Grosbeak (p. 140) both lack the yellow body plumage.

breeding

Quick I.D.: smaller than a robin. *Breeding male:* yellow body with contrasting black wings and tail; red on head. *Non-breeding male* and *Female:* olive-yellow overall.
Size: 6¹/₂–7¹/₂ in.

Jan Feb Mar Apr May Jun Jul Aug Sept Oct Nov Dec

Horned Lark
Eremophila alpestris

From the seashore to mountain tops and arctic tundra, no other bird in North America spans such diverse habitats. Horned Larks are birds of open, treeless country. In these often bleak environments, Horned Larks are able to find the shelter and food that evades most other birds.

These ground-loving birds breed on the remaining coastal plains in the San Diego region. Here, too, from November to February, mountain- and northern-nesting larks congregate among the residing hosts. There are many subspecies of larks represented in southern California at this time, and the slight differences in plumage can allow for some assumptions about the breeding destination of the birds. The resident birds are somewhat paler than those destined for the Colorado desert, whereas an intermediate form is likely to breed in the Mojave desert. Whatever their destination, Horned Larks instill motion and interest to our backroads, fields and coastlines.

Similar Species: American Pipit (p. 121) lacks the facial pattern and the black outer tail feathers.

Quick I.D.: sparrow-sized.
Male: small black 'horns' (often not raised); black line running under eye from bill to cheek; light yellow to white face; dull brown upperparts; black breast band; dark tail with white outer tail feathers; light throat.
Female: less distinctive head patterning; duller plumage overall.
Size: 7–8 in.

Jan	Feb	Mar	Apr	May	Jun	Jul	Aug	Sept	Oct	Nov	Dec

Northern Mockingbird

Mimus polyglottos

Once largely restricted to desert scrub and chaparral in southern California, the Northern Mockingbird has expanded its range northward and westward in the wake of agricultural and urban development. It has adapted well to the broken forests and urban fruit-bearing bushes so common in our region, and it is now a common sight in San Diego.

The Northern Mockingbird is perhaps best known for its ability to mimic sounds. It can expertly imitate other birds, barking dogs and even musical instruments. So accurate is the mimicry that sonographic analysis often cannot detect differences between the original version and the mockingbird's.

Similar Species: Loggerhead Shrike (p. 123) has a black mask and a stout, hooked bill.

Jan Feb Mar Apr May Jun Jul Aug Sept Oct Nov Dec

Quick I.D.: robin-sized; black wings and tail with white patches; gray head and back; light underparts; long tail; thin bill; sexes similar.

Size: 10–11 in.

California Thrasher
Toxostoma redivivum

A scratcher and a digger, the California Thrasher rustles through fallen leaves with a vigor matched by few birds. In the dense underbrush of chaparral, the thrasher's activities are most often encountered by our ears rather than our eyes. Using its long, downcurved bill, the thrasher noisily digs and tosses leaves, but it is not easily seen. Even if you crouch and peer low under the dense bushes, the thrasher will only give you a quick glimpse of its long tail and peachy underparts as a reward. A proactive approach may produce the best results: a thrasher readily responds to squeaking and pishing, often peeking curiously out of its sheltered sanctuary.

True to its name, the California Thrasher is found almost exclusively in this state. In spite of this limited distribution, it is a fairly common resident in foothills and natural valleys. While walking trails through chaparral, pay special attention to the noises at ground level: a meeting with a California Thrasher may just result.

Similar Species: California Towhee (p. 126) is much smaller and lacks the long, downcurved bill.

Quick I.D.: dove-sized; dark upperparts; peachy belly and undertail coverts; long, down-curved bill; light tan eyebrow; sexes similar.
Size: 11–13 in.

Jan Feb Mar Apr May Jun Jul Aug Sept Oct Nov Dec

American Pipit

Anthus rubescens

breeding

American Pipits certainly earn their winter vacations in southern California: they breed in some of the harshest environments in North America. Once they return from the arctic and alpine tundra in Alaska and British Columbia in fall, pipits can be seen along shorelines and open areas. Although the climate may have changed, their disdain for trees and other vegetation transcends their geographic location.

While visiting just about any open field or seashore during the winter months, be sure to keep an eye open for the American Pipit. Like many shorebirds and blackbirds, the pipit forages almost exclusively in damp areas on the ground. The best way to identify this drab dresser is to watch its tail—if you are looking at an American Pipit, its tail will bob rhythmically.

Similar Species: Savannah Sparrow (p. 127) has yellow lores and light legs and is stockier overall.

Quick I.D.: sparrow-sized; brown-gray upperparts; lightly streaked underparts; dark tail with white outer tail feathers; bobs tail; slim bill; black legs; sexes similar.

Size: 6¹/₂–7 in.

Jan Feb Mar Apr May Jun Jul Aug Sept Oct Nov Dec

Cedar Waxwing
Bombycilla cedrorum

A faint, high-pitched trill is often your first clue that waxwings are around. Search the treetops to see these cinnamon-crested birds as they dart out in quick bursts, snacking on flying insects. Cedar Waxwings are found in many habitats throughout the San Diego area, wherever ripe berries provide abundant food supplies.

Cedar Waxwings are most often seen in large flocks in late spring, when they congregate on fruit trees and quickly eat all the berries. Some people remember these visits not only for the birds' beauty, but because fermentation of the fruit occasionally renders the flock flightless from intoxication.

Similar Species: Oak Titmouse (p. 99) has no yellow on its belly or tail.

Quick I.D.: smaller than a robin; fine, pale brown plumage; small crest; black mask; yellow belly wash; yellow-tipped tail; light undertail coverts; shiny red (waxy-looking) droplets on wing tips; sexes similar.
Size: 7–8 in.

Jan	Feb	Mar	Apr	May	Jun	Jul	Aug	Sept	Oct	Nov	Dec

Loggerhead Shrike

Lanius ludovicianus

Although a first glance a Loggerhead Shrike may look just like a chunky Northern Mockingbird, this similarity is only superficial. The Loggerhead Shrike is a very special bird in our area: not only is it declining, but also it has behaviors that border on the macabre.

Rather than simply singing to establish territories and attract mates, Loggerhead Shrikes take a rather ghastly approach: they display impaled prey. All about a male's territory in spring you can find dead carcasses of birds, small mammals, insects and reptiles, skewered onto thorns and barbed wire. Although this may not appeal to our refined idea of romance, these actions demonstrate the male's competence to female shrikes. This behavior continues throughout the year; these 'Butcher Birds' impale their prey as a means of storing excess food items during times of plenty. Loggerhead Shrikes have extremely good memories: birds have been observed retrieving stored prey up to eight months later.

Similar Species: Northern Mockingbird (p. 119) lacks the black mask and has larger white wing patches.

Quick I.D.: robin-sized; black mask; dark gray crown and back; black wings and tail; light gray underparts; hooked bill; sexes similar. *In flight:* white patches in wings and outer tail; quick wing beats. *Immature:* paler, slightly barred plumage.

Size: 9 in.

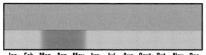

Jan Feb Mar Apr May Jun Jul Aug Sept Oct Nov Dec

European Starling

Sturnus vulgaris

In 1942, 52 years after their intentional release in New York's Central Park, European Starlings began to establish themselves in California. Less than a decade later, flocks of more than one million birds were being reported. Today, European Starlings are one of the most common birds in our area. Their presence is highlighted by astonishing numbers roosting communally during the winter months.

Unfortunately, the expansion of starlings has come at the expense of many of our native birds, including the Purple Martin and the Western Bluebird, which are unable to defend nest cavities against the aggressive starling. While not all birdwatchers are pleased with the presence of this foreigner to our area, starlings have become a permanent fixture in the bird community. If residents are unable to find joy in this bird's mimicry and flocking, they may take some comfort from the fact that starlings now provide a reliable and stable food source for woodland hawks and the Peregrine Falcon.

Similar Species: All blackbirds (pp. 132 & 134–35) have long tails and black bills. Purple Martin has a short bill.

breeding

Quick I.D.: smaller than a robin; short tail; sexes similar. *Breeding:* dark, glossy plumage; long, yellow bill. *Non-breeding:* dark bill; spotty plumage. *Juvenile:* brown upperparts; gray-brown underparts; brown bill.
Size: 8–9 in.

Jan Feb Mar Apr May Jun Jul Aug Sept Oct Nov Dec

Spotted Towhee
Pipilo maculatus

♂

This large, colorful sparrow is most often heard before it is seen, scratching away leaves and debris in the dense understorey. It is a common year-round resident in many local parks and shrubby backyards. Deep in the shadows of shrubs, the Spotted Towhee's sharp, nasal *t'wee* call and its *Here Here Here PLEASE!* song identify this secretive sparrow.

To best observe this bird, which was formerly grouped with the Eastern Towhee—together they were known as the Rufous-sided Towhee—learn a few birding tricks. Squeaking and pishing are irresistible for towhees, which will quickly pop out from the cover to investigate the curious noise.

Similar Species: American Robin (p. 109) is larger and has no white on its breast. Dark-eyed Junco (p. 131) is smaller and has white outer tail feathers. Black-headed Grosbeak (p. 140) has an orange breast, a larger bill and a shorter tail.

Quick I.D.: smaller than a robin; black head; rufous-colored flanks; spotted back; white outer tail feathers; white underparts; red eyes. *Male:* black head, breast and upperparts. *Female:* reddish-brown head, breast and upperparts.
Size: 8–9 in.

Jan Feb Mar Apr May Jun Jul Aug Sept Oct Nov Dec

California Towhee

Pipilo crissalis

The sharp metallic *chip* note of the California Towhee bursts from bushes and shrubs in a proclamation of this bird's territory. California Towhees are strongly territorial, and in the dense vegetation of backyards, city parks, coastal scrub and broken chaparral communities, pairs establish and aggressively defend their territories against their neighbors.

California Towhees are year-round residents in the San Diego area. These woodland-edge specialists build their bulky nests fairly low to the ground in a bush, often in well-vegetated parks and backyards. They peck and scratch for seeds on the bare ground in open areas, and if a pair is separated while foraging, they re-establish contact by squealing atop a bush. Once reunited, they bob rhythmically to reaffirm their life-long bond.

Until recently, the California Towhee and the Canyon Towhee were lumped together (and collectively called the Brown Towhee), but recent studies have shown that the birds living in lowland California are a separate species.

Similar Species: California Thrasher (p. 120) has a long, curved bill, a white throat and a light eyebrow. Female Brewer's Blackbird (p. 134) lacks the rusty undertail coverts and the conical bill.

Quick I.D.: robin-sized; brown upperparts; light brown underparts; rusty undertail coverts; brown crown; buffy throat with a broken, black 'necklace'; short, stout, conical bill; yellow legs; long tail; sexes similar.
Juvenile: streaked underparts.
Size: 8¹/₂–10 in.

Jan Feb Mar Apr May Jun Jul Aug Sept Oct Nov Dec

Savannah Sparrow
Passerculus sandwichensis

The Savannah Sparrow is one of the most widespread birds in North America. Because of its large distribution, several subspecies occur across North America, including southern California's own 'Belding's Sparrow.' This endangered subspecies of the Savannah Sparrow breeds in semi-open areas along the coast and in grasslands in lowland areas. As with so many lowland-breeding species, urban development has reduced the amount of available habitat to south San Diego Bay.

The Savannah Sparrow resorts to flight only as a last alternative—it prefers to run swiftly and inconspicuously through long grass—and it is most often seen darting across roads and open fields. Its dull brown plumage and streaked breast conceal it perfectly in the long grasses of meadows and roadsides.

The Savannah Sparrow's distinctive buzzy trill—*tea-tea-tea-teeea today*—and the yellow patch in front of each eye are the best ways to distinguish it from the many other shrubland sparrows.

Similar Species: Lincoln's Sparrow has a buffy head and breast and a wren-like song.

Quick I.D.: small sparrow; streaked underparts and upperparts; mottled brown above; dark cheek; no white outer tail feathers; many have yellow lores; sexes similar.

Size: 5–6 in.

Jan Feb Mar Apr May Jun Jul Aug Sept Oct Nov Dec

Fox Sparrow
Passerella iliaca

The Fox Sparrow is a winter visitor in San Diego's thickets and brambles; it is most common from October through April. Like many other sparrows that winter in this habitat, the Fox Sparrow is appreciated for its voice more than for its plumage. Although the subtlety of the Fox Sparrow's plumage is beautiful, its voice overshadows its appearance. During late winter, sit and wait near tangles and brush piles in parks; listen as the Fox Sparrow repeatedly belts out its distinctive musical question: *all I have is what's here dear, will-you-will-you take-it?*

Similar Species: Song Sparrow (p. 129) has a different song and much lighter plumage. Lincoln's Sparrow has weaker breast streaks. Hermit Thrush (p. 108) has a smaller bill and thinner breast spots. Swainson's Thrush has a pale eye ring and olive upperparts.

Quick I.D.: large sparrow; heavy breast streaks form dark breast; brown plumage; very dark overall; sexes similar.
Size: 6¹/₂–7 in.

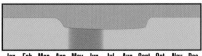

Jan Feb Mar Apr May Jun Jul Aug Sept Oct Nov Dec

Song Sparrow
Melospiza melodia

The Song Sparrow's drab, heavily streaked plumage doesn't prepare you for its symphonic song, which stands among those of the great songsters in complexity and rhythm. This commonly heard bird seems to be singing *hip-hip-hip hooray boys, the spring is here again.*

This year-round resident is encountered in a wide variety of habitats: Song Sparrows are easily found in all seasons among marshes, thickets, blackberry brambles, weedy fields and woodland edges. Although these birds are most easily identified by their grayish streaks while perched, flying birds will characteristically pump their tails.

Similar Species: Fox Sparrow (p. 128) is very heavily streaked and has a different song. Savannah Sparrow (p. 127) and Lincoln's Sparrow have weaker breast streaks.

Jan Feb Mar Apr May Jun Jul Aug Sept Oct Nov Dec

Quick I.D.: mid-sized sparrow; heavy breast streaks form central breast spot; brown-red plumage; striped head; sexes similar.

Size: 6–7 in.

White-crowned Sparrow

Zonotrichia leucophrys

White-crowned Sparrows are usually seen foraging on the ground or in low shrubs. They normally feed a short distance from thickets and tall grasses, always maintaining a quick escape path into the safety of concealing vegetation. Overwintering White-crowned Sparrows often feed at backyard feeders. They are very persistent singers, and their songs can be heard well into the evening hours.

These common year-round residents of southern California represent a distinct subspecies of the White-crowned Sparrow. San Diego's White-crowns tend to have white lores, brown upperparts and gray-brown underparts.

Similar Species: Golden-crowned Sparrow has a golden-yellow crown. White-throated Sparrow (uncommon in San Diego) has yellow lores and a clear white throat.

Quick I.D.: large sparrow; striped, black-and-white crown; pink bill; unstreaked breast; brown upperparts; gray-brown underparts; sexes similar.
Immature: no crown; buffy-olive upperparts; faint yellow underparts.
Size: 5¹/₂–7 in.

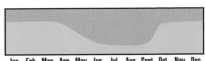

Jan Feb Mar Apr May Jun Jul Aug Sept Oct Nov Dec

Dark-eyed Junco

Junco hyemalis

♂

While Americans east of the Rockies do have Dark-eyed Juncos, only West Coast residents have the splashy race with the black hood and tail and the pinkish body, which is sometimes called the Oregon Junco.

Many Dark-eyed Juncos breed in city parks, and they are abundant winter visitors throughout the San Diego area. The Dark-eyed Junco is a ground dweller, and it is frequently seen as it flushes from the undergrowth along wooded park trails. The distinctive, white outer tail feathers will flash in alarm as it flies down a narrow path before disappearing into a thicket. The junco's distinctive smacking call and its habit of double-scratching at forest litter also help identify it. Juncos are common guests at birdfeeders, and they usually pick up the scraps that have fallen to the ground.

Similar Species: Spotted Towhee (p. 125) is larger and has white 'flaking' on its back. Brown-headed Cowbird (p. 135) lacks the white outer tail feathers.

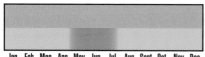

Jan Feb Mar Apr May Jun Jul Aug Sept Oct Nov Dec

Quick I.D.: mid-sized sparrow; black hood; brown back; pinkish sides; pink bill; white outer tail feathers; white belly; sexes similar.
Size: 5–6¹/₂ in.

Red-winged Blackbird
Agelaius phoeniceus

From March through July, no marsh is free from the loud calls and bossy, aggressive nature of the Red-winged Blackbird. A springtime walk around any extensive cattail marsh will be accompanied by this bird's loud, raspy and persistent *konk-a-reee* or *eat my CHEEEzies* song.

The male's bright red shoulders are his most important tool in the strategic and intricate displays he uses to defend his territory from rivals and to attract a mate. In experiments, males whose red shoulders were painted black soon lost their territories to rivals they had previously defeated. The female's interest lies not in the individual combatants, but in nesting habitat, and a male who can successfully defend a large area of dense cattails will breed with many females. After the females have built their concealed nests and laid their eggs, the male continues his persistent vigil.

Similar Species: Tricolored Blackbird has dark red shoulder patches with white trim. Brewer's Blackbird (p. 134) and Brown-headed Cowbird (p. 135) both lack the red shoulder patches.

Quick I.D.: smaller than a robin. *Male:* all-black plumage; large red patch on each shoulder. *Female:* brown overall; heavily streaked; hint of red on shoulder.
Size: 7¹/₂–9¹/₂ in.

Jan Feb Mar Apr May Jun Jul Aug Sept Oct Nov Dec

Western Meadowlark

Sturnella neglecta

Western Meadowlarks commonly breed in grasslands around the San Diego area, but the occurrence of this open-country bird is most notable during the winter months. Their fiercely defended summer solitude and territoriality is abandoned in winter, and flocks of up to 40 meadowlarks can be seen wheeling over open fields, pastures and river deltas, taking off and alighting in unison.

The Western Meadowlark is well adapted to wide open spaces: its long legs carry it quickly through the grass, and its mottled color blends in with the often drab surroundings. In anticipation of their spring departure, Western Meadowlarks may begin singing in March, offering up their melodies to the fields in which they wintered.

Similar Species: None.

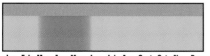

Jan Feb Mar Apr May Jun Jul Aug Sept Oct Nov Dec

Quick I.D.: robin-sized; mottled brown upperparts; black 'V' on breast; yellow throat and belly; white outer tail feathers; striped head; sexes similar.

Size: 8–10 in.

Brewer's Blackbird

Euphagus cyanocephalus

These small blackbirds are common throughout our urban areas; they commonly squabble with pigeons and starlings for leftover scraps of food. In the San Diego area, this species is most abundant in rural pasturelands, in river valleys and along highways, where they are observed strutting confidently in defiance of nearby speeding vehicles.

Brewer's Blackbirds are bold, and they allow us to easily and intimately observe them. By studying the behavior of several birds within a flock, you can determine the hierarchy of the flock as it is perceived by the birds themselves.

The feathers of Brewer's Blackbirds, which superficially appear black, actually show an iridescent quality as reflected rainbows of sunlight move along the feather shafts.

Similar Species: Male Red-winged Blackbird (p. 132) has a red patch on each wing. Brown-headed Cowbird (p. 135) has a shorter tail and a stout bill, and the male has a brown hood.

Quick I.D.: robin-sized; long tail; slim bill. *Male:* all-black, slightly iridescent plumage; light yellow eyes. *Female:* brown overall; brown eyes.
Size: 8–10 in.

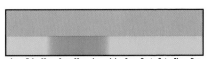

Jan Feb Mar Apr May Jun Jul Aug Sept Oct Nov Dec

Brown-headed Cowbird

Molothrus ater

The Brown-headed Cowbird has firmly established itself within the matrix of the region's bird life. This gregarious bird is very common in city parks during the summer months. During winter, it commonly mixes with other blackbirds in outlying agricultural areas.

The Brown-headed Cowbird is infamous for being a nest parasite—female cowbirds do not incubate their own eggs, but instead lay them in the nests of songbirds. Cowbird eggs have a short incubation period, and the cowbird chicks often hatch before the host songbird's own chicks. Many songbirds will continue to feed the fast-growing cowbird chick, even after it has grown larger than the songbird. In its efforts to get as much food as possible, a cowbird chick may squeeze the host's own young out of the nest. The populations of some songbirds have been reduced in part by the activities of the Brown-headed Cowbird, but other songbird species recognize the foreign egg, and they either eject it from their nest or they build a new nest.

Similar Species: Brewer's Blackbird (p. 134) has a long tail and a thin bill, and the male has a purple head and yellow eyes.

Quick I.D.: smaller than a robin. *Male:* metallic-looking, glossy black plumage; soft brown head; dark eyes. *Female:* brownish gray overall; dark eyes; slight breast streaks.

Size: 6–8 in.

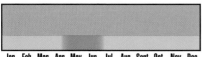

Jan Feb Mar Apr May Jun Jul Aug Sept Oct Nov Dec

Bullock's Oriole

Icterus bullockii

Although it is a common summer resident of city parks and wooded valleys, the Bullock's Oriole is seldom seen. Unlike the American Robin, which inhabits the human domain of shrubs and lawns, the Bullock's Oriole nests and feeds in the tallest deciduous trees available. The vacant nest, which is easily seen on bare trees in fall, is often the only indication that a pair of orioles summered in an area. This bird's hanging, six-inch-deep, pouch-like nest is deceptively strong. It is principally made by the female, which incubates the four to five eggs for approximately two weeks.

The male Bullock's Oriole's striking, Halloween-like, black-and-orange plumage flashes like embers amidst the dense foliage of the tree-tops, while its slow purposeful *Peter Peter here here Peter Peter* song drips to the forest floor.

Similar Species: Western Tanager (p. 117) has yellow plumage, a relatively shorter tail and a heavier bill.

Quick I.D.: smaller than a robin. *Male:* brilliant orange belly flanks, outer tail feathers and rump; black crown, upper back, wings, bib and central tail feathers; large white wing patch; black eye line. *Female:* yellow-green upperparts; yellow throat.
Size: 7–8 in.

Jan Feb Mar Apr May Jun Jul Aug Sept Oct Nov Dec

House Finch
Carpodacus mexicanus

The House Finch is
one of the earliest voices to
announce the coming of spring.
These common city and country birds
sing their melodies from backyards, parks,
ivy vines and telephone lines.

During the 1920s and 1930s, these birds, native to the American South-
west, were popular cage birds, and they were sold across the continent as
Hollywood Finches. Illegal releases of the caged birds from Long Island,
New York, has resulted in the population east of the Rockies. In San
Diego, House Finches have spread and multiplied on the heels of residen-
tial developments.

Similar Species: Male Purple Finch is raspberry-colored and has
unstreaked undertail coverts, and the female has a brown cheek contrasting with a white eyebrow and a mustache stripe.

Quick I.D.: sparrow-sized;
squared tail. *Male:* deep red
forehead, eyebrow and throat;
buffy streaked belly; brown
cheek; streaked undertail
coverts. *Female:* brown overall;
streaked underparts; brown
face; no eyebrow.
Size: 5–5½ in.

Jan Feb Mar Apr May Jun Jul Aug Sept Oct Nov Dec

Lesser Goldfinch
Carduelis psaltria

Searching through flocks of finches in southern California often rewards the viewer with the sight of the day-night plumage of the male Lesser Goldfinch. These birds frequently associate with Pine Siskins and American Goldfinch flocks foraging for thistle or other weed seeds in overgrown fields.

The voice of the Lesser Goldfinch is made up of various twittering notes, often copied from neighboring species. It seems as though no two birds sing the exact same complicated song, but with a little practice, the quality and tone of their voices is sufficient for identification. It is thought that female Lesser Goldfinches are attracted by the males' songs rather than their dressy style. First year males, still without the contrasting plumage of the mature males, are often just as successful as their older peers in finding mates. Once paired, the birds built a nest in a shrub where the female will incubate four to five eggs for 12 days.

Similar Species: American Goldfinch (p. 139) has yellow plumage, white undertail coverts and an orange bill.

Quick I.D.: smaller than a sparrow; yellow green body; dark wings and tail; white patch in wings; dark legs. *Male:* black cap. *Female:* lacks black cap.
Size: 4¹/₂–5¹/₂ in.

Jan Feb Mar Apr May Jun Jul Aug Sept Oct Nov Dec

American Goldfinch
Carduelis tristis

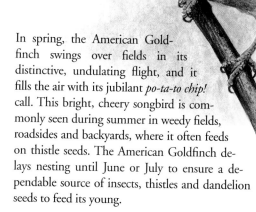

♂

breeding

In spring, the American Gold-finch swings over fields in its distinctive, undulating flight, and it fills the air with its jubilant *po-ta-to chip!* call. This bright, cheery songbird is commonly seen during summer in weedy fields, roadsides and backyards, where it often feeds on thistle seeds. The American Goldfinch delays nesting until June or July to ensure a dependable source of insects, thistles and dandelion seeds to feed its young.

The American Goldfinch is a common backyard bird in parts of the San Diego area, and it can easily be attracted to feeding stations that offer a supply of niger seed. Unfortunately, goldfinches are easily bullied at feeders by larger sparrows and finches. Only goldfinches and Pine Siskins invert for food, however, so a special finch feeder with openings below the perches is ideal for ensuring a steady stream of these 'wild canaries.'

Similar Species: Yellow Warbler (p. 112) and Wilson's Warbler (p. 116) do not have black on their forehead or wings. Evening Grosbeak is much larger.

Quick I.D.: smaller than a sparrow. *Breeding male:* black forehead, wings and tail; canary-yellow body; wings show white in flight. *Female* and *Non-breeding male:* no black on forehead; yellow-green overall; black wings and tail.
Size: 4^1/$_2$–5^1/$_2$ in.

Jan Feb Mar Apr May Jun Jul Aug Sept Oct Nov Dec

Black-headed Grosbeak

Pheucticus melanocephalus

The male Black-headed Grosbeak has a brilliant voice to match his Halloween plumage, and he flaunts his song in treetop performances. This common songster's boldness does not go unnoticed by the appreciative birding community, which eagerly anticipates the males' annual spring concerts. Female grosbeaks lack the formal dress, but they share their partners' musical talents.

This neotropical migrant nests in mature deciduous forests and mixed oak-conifer forests, such as those found in less developed urban areas and at higher elevations. Whether the nest is tended by the male or female, the developing young are continually introduced into the world of song by the brooding parent.

Similar Species: Spotted Towhee (p. 125) has a smaller bill and a longer tail. Female Purple Finch and female sparrows (pp. 127–30) are generally smaller.

Quick I.D.: smaller than a robin; light-colored, conical bill. *Male:* black head, wings and tail; orange body; white wing patches. *Female:* finely streaked with brown; white eyebrow; light throat.
Size: 7–8¹/₂ in.

Jan Feb Mar Apr May Jun Jul Aug Sept Oct Nov Dec

Lazuli Bunting
Passerina amoena

♂

While hiking through the shrubby habitat of the Lazuli Bunting, you might soon notice the complexities of the males' songs. Neighboring males copy and learn from one another, producing 'song territories.' Each male within a song territory has personal variation to *swip-swip-swip zu zu ee, see see sip see see*, producing his own acoustic fingerprint.

Lazuli Buntings are widespread throughout our area during summer, popping out of dense bushes in mountains and foothills, often near water. They build a small nest cup low to the ground, in an upright crotch in a shrubby tangle.

Once nesting duties are complete, these buntings are quick to leave our area, beginning their exodus in August after a partial molt. They owe their name to the colorful gemstone lapis lazuli. (The accepted pronunciation of the name is 'LAZZ-you-lie,' but variations are as common as the variety in the bird's own song.)

Similar Species: Western Bluebird (p. 107) is larger but has a slimmer body and lacks the wing bars.

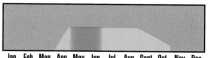

Jan Feb Mar Apr May Jun Jul Aug Sept Oct Nov Dec

Quick I.D.: sparrow-sized. *Male:* turquoise blue hood and rump; white breast; white belly; dark wings and tail; two white wing bars. *Female:* soft brown overall; hints of blue on rump.
Size: 5¹/₂ in.

House Sparrow

Passer domesticus

This common backyard bird often confuses novice birdwatchers, because females and immatures can be very nondescript. The male is relatively conspicuous—he has a black bib, a gray cap and white lines trailing down from his mouth (as though he has spilled milk on himself)—and he sings a continuous series of *cheep-cheep-cheep*s. The best field mark for the female, apart from her pale eyebrows, is that there are no distinctive field marks.

The House Sparrow was introduced to North America in the 1850s to control insects. Although this familiar bird can consume great quantities of insects, the majority of its diet is seeds, and it has become somewhat of a pest. The House Sparrow's aggressive nature usurps several native songbirds from nesting cavities, and its boldness often drives other birds away from backyard feeders. The House Sparrow and the European Starling are now two of the most common birds in cities and on farms, and they are a constant reminder of the negative impact of human introductions on natural systems.

Similar Species: Male is distinctive. Female is similar to female sparrows (pp. 127–30) and female finches (p. 137).

Quick I.D.: mid-sized sparrow; brownish-gray belly. *Male:* black throat; gray forehead; white jowls; chestnut nape. *Female:* plain; pale eyebrow; mottled wings.
Size: 5¹/₂–6¹/₂ in.

Jan Feb Mar Apr May Jun Jul Aug Sept Oct Nov Dec

Watching Birds

Identifying your first new bird can be so satisfying that you just might become addicted to birdwatching. Luckily, birdwatching does not have to be expensive. It all hinges on how involved in this hobby you want to get. Setting up a simple backyard feeder is an easy way to get to know the birds sharing your neighborhood, and some people simply find bird-watching a pleasant way to complement a nightly walk with the dog or a morning commute into work.

Many people enjoy going to urban parks and feeding the wild birds that have become accustomed to humans. This activity provides people with intimate contact with urban-dwelling birds, but remember that birdseed, or better yet the birds' natural food items, are much healthier for the birds than bread and crackers. As a spokesperson for the animals' health, kindly remind 'bread tossers' of the implications of their actions.

SEASONS OF BIRDWATCHING

Spring

Springtime in San Diego is a prolonged affair. Beginning as early as January, winter residents, such as the Red-naped Sapsucker and Tree Swallow, are already embarking on travels northward, while one morning a Yellow Warbler or Winter Wren might suddenly decide to sing. Birders in San Diego County are treated to a sudden influx of birdlife, a trend that lasts into the summer months.

Coastal activity is hectic as flocks of loons, brants and scoters pass through the area. Tremendous flocks of shorebirds may be seen, and species such as the Caspian Tern and Cliff Swallow hastily set up their nesting grounds. Other species, such as the Lazuli Bunting, Nashville Warbler and Western Tanager, pass briefly through the area; although these species aren't here for good, the San Diego area provides valuable habitat for their short but important stays.

Summer

Summertime finds most birds busy tending to their families and less likely to put on a show for human observers. Singing gives way to more serious nest-building and incubation. Comfortable with the hot and dry weather, such nesting residents as the Bullock's Oriole and Hutton's Vireo raise their broods in the native black oak and sycamore groves. San Diego's beautiful riparian woodlands are home to such breeding species as the Red-shouldered Hawk, Nuttall's Woodpecker and Yellow-breasted Chat. In July and August shorebirds are once again retreating south; perhaps this is a good time for birders to visit San Diego's cooler coastal areas. Southern California summers are indeed a pleasure to discover.

Fall

Fall migration is an extraordinary event in southern California. From as early as June or July, and extending into October and November, this season has more bird traffic than

any other time of the year. Large numbers of shorebirds and freshwater ducks travel through the area. Some are just passing through, but others may decide to settle for the winter season. By September or October, the trees and shrubs of San Diego County are once again alive with the constant flitting of songbirds. The unique geographical features of southern California funnel many songbirds westward; during the fall months these birds are periodically seen in large numbers.

Winter

Winter in the San Diego area provides valuable habitat and a healthy food supply for a plethora of birdlife. Birders will find that summer sightings pale in comparison to those in winter. Loons, grebes and water-

fowl, frozen out of their summer breeding grounds, ride out winter on the open ocean, calm bays or lakes and ponds in the area. Many birds descend from southern California's high mountain slopes; other species, such as the Cedar Waxwing, can be can be seen traveling through residential areas in search of succulent berries and other tasty treats. Birdfeeders are very busy at this time of year and are pleasurable additions to any neighborhood yard.

BIRDING OPTICS

Most people who are interested in birdwatching will eventually buy binoculars. They help you identify key bird characteristics, such as plumage and bill color, and they also help you identify other birders! Birdwatchers are a friendly sort, and a chat among birders is all part of the experience.

You'll use your binoculars often, so select a model that will contribute to the quality of your birdwatching experience—they don't have to be expensive. If you need help deciding which model is right for you, talk to other birdwatchers or to someone at your local nature center. Many models are available, and when shopping for binoculars it's important to keep two things in mind: weight and magnification.

One of the first things you'll notice about binoculars (apart from the price extremes) is that they all have two numbers associated with them (8x40, for example). The first number, which is always the smallest, is the magnification (how large the bird will appear), while the second is the size (in millimeters) of the objective lens (the larger end). It may seem important at first to get the highest magnification possible, but a reasonable magnification of 7x–8x is optimal for all-purpose birding, because it draws you fairly close to most birds without causing too much shaking. Some shaking happens to everyone; to overcome it, rest the binoculars against a support, such as a partner's shoulder or a tree.

The size of the objective lens is really a question of birding conditions and weight. Because wider lenses (40–50 mm) will bring in more light, these are preferred for birding in low-light situations (like before sunrise or after sunset). If these aren't the conditions that you will be pursuing, a light model that has an objective lens diameter of less than 30 mm may be the right choice. Because binoculars tend to become heavy after hanging around your neck all day, the compact models are becoming increasingly popular. If you have a model that is heavy, you can purchase a strap that redistributes part of the weight to the shoulders and lower back.

Another valuable piece of equipment is a spotting scope. It is very useful when you are trying to sight waterfowl, shorebirds or soaring raptors, but it is really of no use if you are intent on seeing forest birds. A good spotting scope has a magnification of around 40x. It has a sturdy tripod or a window mount for the car. Be wary of second-hand models of telescopes, as they are designed for seeing stars, and their magnifications are too great for birdwatching. One of the advantages of having a scope is that you will be able to see far-off birds, such as overwintering waterfowl on the ocean, or birds in migration, such as shorebirds and raptors. By setting up in one spot (or by not even leaving your car) you can observe faraway flocks that would be little more than specks in your binoculars.

With these simple pieces of equipment (none of which is truly essential) and this handy field guide, anyone can enjoy birds in their area. Many birds are difficult to see because they stay hidden in treetops, but you can learn to identify them by their songs. After experiencing the thrill of a couple of hard-won identifications, you will find yourself taking your binoculars on walks, drives and trips to the beach and cabin. As rewards accumulate with experience, you may find the books and photos piling up and your trips being planned just to see birds!

BIRDING BY EAR

Sometimes, bird listening can be more effective than bird watching. The technique of birding by ear is gaining popularity, because listening for birds can be more efficient, productive and rewarding than waiting for a visual confirmation. Birds have distinctive songs that they use to resolve territorial disputes, and sound is therefore a useful way to identify species. It is particularly useful when trying to watch some of the smaller forest-dwelling birds. Their size and often indistinct plumage can make a visual search of the forest canopy frustrating. To facilitate auditory searches, catchy paraphrases are included in the descriptions of many of the birds. If the paraphrase just doesn't seem to work for you (they are often a personal thing) be creative and try to find one that fits. By spending time playing the song over in your head, fitting words to it, the voices of birds soon become as familiar as the voices of family members. Many excellent CDs and tapes are available at bookstores and wild-bird stores for the songs of the birds in your area.

BIRDFEEDERS

They're messy, they can be costly, and they're sprouting up in neighborhoods everywhere. Feeding birds has become a common pastime in residential communities all over North America. Although the concept is fairly straightforward, as with anything else involving birds, feeders can become quite elaborate.

The great advantage to feeding birds is that neighborhood chickadees, jays, juncos and finches are enticed into regular visits. Don't expect birds to arrive at your feeder as soon as you set it up; it may take weeks for a few regulars to incorporate your yard into their daily routine. As the popularity of your feeder grows, the number of visiting birds will increase and more species will arrive. You will notice that your feeder is busier during the winter months, when natural foods are less abundant. You can increase the odds of a good avian turnout by using a variety of feeders and seeds. When a number of birds habitually visit your yard, maintaining the feeder becomes a responsibility, because the birds may begin to rely on it as a regular food source.

Larger birds tend to enjoy feeding on platforms or on the ground; smaller birds are comfortable on hanging seed dispensers. Certain seeds tend to attract specific birds; nature centers and wild-bird supply stores are the best places to ask how to attract a favorite species. It's mainly seed eaters that are attracted to backyards; some birds have no interest in feeders. Only the most committed birdwatcher will try to attract birds that are insect eaters, berry eaters or, in some extreme cases, scavengers!

The location of the feeder may influence the amount of business it receives from the neighborhood birds. Because birds are wild, they are instinctively wary, and they are unlikely to visit an area where they may come under attack. When putting up your feeder, think like a bird. A good, clear view with convenient escape routes is always appreciated. Cats like birdfeeders that are close to the ground and within pouncing distance from a bush; obviously, birds don't. Above all, a birdfeeder should be in view of a favorite window, where you can sit and enjoy the rewarding interaction of your appreciative feathered guests.

Glossary

accipiter: a forest hawk (genus *Accipiter*); characterized by a long tail and short, rounded wings; feeds mostly on birds.

brood: *n*. a family of young from one hatching; *v*. to sit on eggs so as to hatch them.

coniferous: cone-producing trees, usually softwood evergreens (e.g., spruce, pine, fir).

corvid: a member of the crow family (Corvidae); includes crows, jays, magpies and ravens.

covey: a brood or flock of partridges, quails or grouse.

crop: an enlargement of the esophagus, serving as a storage structure and (in pigeons) has glands which produce secretions.

dabbling: foraging technique used by ducks, where the head and neck are submerged but the body and tail remain on the water's surface.

dabbling duck: a duck that forages by dabbling; it can usually walk easily on land, it can take off without running, and it has a brightly colored speculum; includes Mallards, Gadwalls, teals and others.

deciduous: a tree that loses its leaves annually (e.g., oak, maple, aspen, birch).

dimorphism: the existence of two distinct forms of a species, such as between the sexes.

eclipse: the dull, female-like plumage that male ducks briefly acquire after molting from their breeding plumage.

elbow patches: dark spots at the bend of the outstretched wing, seen from below.

flycatching: feeding behavior where a bird leaves a perch, snatches an insect in mid-air, and returns to their previous perch; also known as 'hawking.'

fledgling: a young chick that has just acquired its permanent flight feathers, but is still dependent on its parents.

flushing: a behavior where frightened birds explode into flight in response to a disturbance.

gape: the size of the mouth opening.

irruption: a sporadic mass migration of birds into a non-breeding area.

larva: a development stage of an animal (usually an invertebrate) that has a different body form from the adult (e.g., caterpillar, maggot).

leading edge: the front edge of the wing as viewed from below.

litter: fallen plant material, such as twigs, leaves and needles, that forms a distinct layer above the soil, especially in forests.

lore: the small patch between the eye and the bill.

molting: the periodic replacement of worn out feathers (often twice a year).

morphology: the science of form and shape.

nape: the back of the neck.

neotropical migrant: a bird that nests in North America, but overwinters in the New World tropics.

niche: an ecological role filled by a species.

open country: a landscape that is primarily not forested.

parasitism: a relationship between two species where one benefits at the expense of the other.

phylogenetics: a method of classifying animals that puts the oldest ancestral groups before those that have arisen more recently.

pishing: making a sound to attract birds by saying *pishhh* as loudly and as wetly as comfortably possible.

polygynous: having a mating strategy where one male breeds with several females.

polyandrous: having a mating strategy where one female breeds with several males.

plucking post: a perch habitually used by an accipiter for plucking feathers from its prey.

raptor: a carnivorous (meat-eating) bird; includes eagles, hawks, falcons and owls.

rufous: rusty red in color.

speculum: a brightly colored patch in the wings of many dabbling ducks.

squeaking: making a sound to attract birds by loudly kissing the back of the hand, or by using a specially design squeaky bird call.

talons: the claws of birds of prey.

understorey: the shrub or thicket layer beneath a canopy of trees.

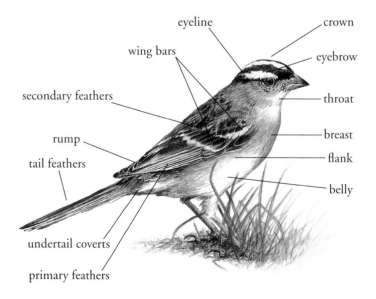

References

American Ornithologists' Union. 1983. *Check-list of North American Birds.* 6th ed. American Ornithologists' Union, Washington, D.C. (and its supplements through July, 1997).

Childs, H.E., Jr. 1993. *Where Birders Go in Southern California.* Rev. ed. Los Angeles Audubon Society, West Hollywood, California.

Ehrlich, P.R., D.S. Dobkin and D. Wheye. 1988. *The Birder's Handbook.* Fireside, New York.

Evans, H.E. 1993. *Pioneer Naturalists: The Discovery and Naming of North American Plants and Animals.* Henry Holt and Company, New York.

Farrand, J., ed. 1983. *The Audubon Society Master Guide to Birding.* Vols. 1–3. Alfred A. Knopf, New York.

Gotch, A.F. 1981. *Birds: Their Latin Names Explained.* Blandford Press, Dorset, England.

Holt, H.R. 1990. *A Birder's Guide to Southern California.* American Birding Association, Colorado Springs.

Mearns, B., and R. Mearns. 1992. *Audubon to Xantus: The Lives of Those Commemorated in North American Bird Names.* Academic Press, San Diego.

National Audubon Society. 1971–1995. *American Birds.* Vols. 25–48.

Peterson, R.T. 1990. *A Field Guide to the Western Birds.* 3rd ed. Houghton Mifflin Co., Boston.

Reader's Digest Association. *Book of North American Birds.* The Reader's Digest Association, Pleasantville, New York.

Robbins, C.S., B. Brunn and H.S. Zim. 1966. *Birds of North America.* Golden Press, New York.

Scott, S.S. 1987. *Field Guide to the Birds of North America.* National Geographic Society, Washington, D.C.

Small, A. 1994. *California Birds: Their Status and Distribution.* Ibis Publishing Co., Vista, Calif.

Stokes, D., and L. Stokes. 1996. *Stokes Field Guide to Birds: Western Region.* Little, Brown and Co., Boston.

Terres, J.K. 1995. *The Audubon Society Encyclopedia of North American Birds.* Wings Books, New York.

Unitt, P. 1984. *The Birds of San Diego County.* San Diego Society of Natural History, San Diego.

Checklist of San Diego Birds

Symbols used in this list are defined as follows:

Seasons

W = Winter (mid-December through February)

Sp = Spring (March through early June)

Su = Summer (mid-June through July)

F = Fall (August through December)

Breeding Status

(B) = Regular breeder (nests each year)

(b) = Irregular breeder (few nesting records for the county; nests infrequently)

(?) = Suspected breeder (nesting confirmation lacking)

(+) = Former breeder (no nesting records in recent years)

Abundance

C = Common to abundant in appropriate habitat (always present, in large numbers)

F = Fairly common (always present, in moderate to small numbers)

U = Uncommon (usually present, in small numbers)

R = Rare (observed in very small numbers, and perhaps not in each year)

X = Extremely rare (fewer than ten records of occurrence in season indicated)

L = Local (restricted to a small portion of the county, or to a few locations, during season indicated)

e = erratic (may occur in substantially larger or smaller numbers than indicated during certain years)

Introduced species (nesting species originally released from captivity) are listed in italics. This checklist does not include 'accidental' species (recorded fewer than 10 times ever in our area and offshore waters). A blank line separates each family of birds on the list.

	W	Sp	Su	F
❑ Red-throated Loon	F	F	R	F
❑ Pacific Loon	F	C	U	F
❑ Common Loon	F	F	R	F
❑ Pied-billed Grebe (B)	F	F	U	F
❑ Horned Grebe	F	F	X	F
❑ Red-necked Grebe	X	X	X	X
❑ Eared Grebe (B)	F	F	X	F
❑ Western Grebe (B)	C	C	U	C
❑ Clark's Grebe (B)	F	F	R	F
❑ Black-footed Albatross		U	U	R
❑ Laysan Albatross	X	X	X	X
❑ Northern Fulmar	Fe	Ue	X	Ue
❑ Pink-footed Shearwater	X	F	F	F
❑ Buller's Shearwater	X		R	F
❑ Sooty Shearwater	R	C	C	C
❑ Short-tailed Shearwater	R	R		R
❑ Black-vented Shearwater	Re	Re	X	Re
❑ Fork-tailed Storm-Petrel	X	X	X	X
❑ Leach's Storm-Petrel		R	R	R
❑ Ashy Storm-Petrel		X	U	U
❑ Black Storm-Petrel			R	U
❑ Least Storm-Petrel			R	F
❑ Red-Billed Tropicbird	RL	RL	RL	RL
❑ American White Pelican	U	R	R	U
❑ Brown Pelican	U	U	C	C
❑ Double-crested Cormorant (B)	C	F	FL	C
❑ Brandt's Cormorant (B)	C	C	FL	C
❑ Pelagic Cormorant	F	F	F	F
❑ Magnificent Frigatebird	R	R	UL	UL
❑ American Bittern	R	R	RL	R
❑ Least Bittern (B)		RL		RL
❑ Great Blue Heron (B)	F	U	U	F
❑ Great Egret (B)	F	U	UL	F
❑ Snowy Egret (B)	F	F	FL	F
❑ Cattle Egret (B)	R	R		R
❑ Green Heron (B)	R	R	RL	R
❑ Black-crowned Night-Heron (B)	F	F	FL	F
❑ White-faced Ibis (B)	RL	U	R	U

	W	Sp	Su	F
❑ Turkey Vulture (B)	F	F	F	F
❑ Tundra Swan	R	X		X
❑ Greater White-fronted Goose	R	X		X
❑ Snow Goose	R	R	X	X
❑ Ross' Goose	X	X	X	X
❑ Brant	R	C	R	U
❑ Canada Goose	F	F	UL	F
❑ Wood Duck (B)	U	U	RL	U
❑ Green-winged Teal	F	F		F
❑ Mallard (B)	C	F	F	C
❑ Northern Pintail (B)	C	U	RL	C
❑ Blue-winged Teal	R	R	X	R
❑ Cinnamon Teal (B)	U	F	UL	F
❑ Northern Shoveler (b)	F	U	RL	F
❑ Gadwall (B)	F	U	UL	F
❑ Eurasian Wigeon	R	X		R
❑ American Wigeon	C	U	X	F
❑ Canvasback	C	F	R	C
❑ Redhead (B)	R	R	R	R
❑ Ring-necked Duck	F	U	X	F
❑ Greater Scaup	C	C	R	C
❑ Lesser Scaup	C	C	R	C
❑ Black Scoter	U	U	R	U
❑ Surf Scoter	C	C	U	C
❑ White-winged Scoter	F	F	R	F
❑ Harlequin Duck	X	X	X	X
❑ Oldsquaw	R	R	X	R
❑ Common Goldeneye	F	F	X	F
❑ Barrow's Goldeneye	X	X	X	X
❑ Bufflehead	C	F	X	F
❑ Hooded Merganser	UL	RL		RL
❑ Common Merganser	R	R	XL	R
❑ Red-breasted Merganser	F	F	R	F
❑ Ruddy Duck (B)	C	F	UL	F
❑ Osprey	R	R	X	R
❑ White-tailed Kite (B)	U	R	RL	U
❑ Bald Eagle	RL	RL	XL	RL
❑ Northern Harrier (B)	U	U	UL	U
❑ Sharp-shinned Hawk	U	U	RL	U
❑ Cooper's Hawk (B)	U	U	U	U
❑ Red-shouldered Hawk (B)	U	U	U	U
❑ Broad-winged Hawk	X	X		R
❑ Swainson's Hawk	R	U	R	U
❑ Red-tailed Hawk (B)	F	F	F	F
❑ Ferruginous Hawk	R	X		R
❑ Rough-legged Hawk	Re	Re		Re
❑ Golden Eagle (+)	R	R	R	R

Species	W	Sp	Su	F
American Kestrel (B)	F	F	F	F
Merlin	U	R		R
Peregrine Falcon (b)	R	R	R	R
Prairie Falcon (B)	R	U	R	U
Ring-necked Pheasant (B)	RL	RL	RL	RL
Wild Turkey (b)	RL	RL	RL	RL
California Quail (B)	C	C		C
Black Rail	X			X
Clapper Rail (B)	XL	XL	XL	XL
Virginia Rail (B)	F	F	U	F
Sora	U	U	XL	U
Common Moorhen (b)	R	RL	RL	R
American Coot (B)	C	C	U	C
Black-bellied Plover	C	C	U	C
Pacific Golden-Plover	R	R	X	R
American Golden-Plover				R
Snowy Plover (B)	UL	RL	RL	UL
Semipalmated Plover	F	F	R	F
Killdeer (B)	C	F	F	C
Black Oystercatcher	UL	UL	UL	UL
Black-necked Stilt (B)	F	F	UL	F
American Avocet (B)	C	C	UL	C
Greater Yellowlegs	F	F	R	F
Lesser Yellowlegs	R	R	X	U
Solitary Sandpiper		X		X
Willet	C	C	U	C
Wandering Tattler	U	U	R	U
Spotted Sandpiper (b)	U	U	RL	U
Whimbrel	F	F	R	F
Long-billed Curlew	F	F	R	F
Marbled Godwit	C	C	U	C
Ruddy Turnstone	U	U	R	U
Black Turnstone	C	C	U	C
Surfbird	F	F	R	F
Red Knot	FL	FL	XL	FL
Sanderling	C	C	U	C
Semipalmated Sandpiper		X	X	R
Western Sandpiper	C	C	U	C
Least Sandpiper	C	C	U	C
Baird's Sandpiper		X	X	R
Pectoral Sandpiper		X	X	R
Dunlin	C	C	X	C
Ruff	RL	X	X	RL

Species	W	Sp	Su	F
Short-billed Dowitcher	C	C	R	C
Long-billed Dowitcher	C	C	R	C
Common Snipe	U	U		U
Wilson's Phalarope		X	R	U
Red-necked Phalarope		C	R	C
Red Phalarope	Ue	Ue	X	Ue
South Polar Skua		X	X	X
Pomarine Jaeger	R	U	R	U
Parasitic Jaeger	X	U	R	U
Long-tailed Jaeger			X	R
Franklin's Gull	X	X	X	X
Bonaparte's Gull	F	C	R	F
Heermann's Gull (b)	R	R	C	C
Mew Gull	C	F		C
Ring-billed Gull	C	C	U	C
California Gull	C	C	F	C
Herring Gull	F	F	X	F
Thayer's Gull	U	U		U
Western Gull (B)	C	C	C	C
Glaucous-winged Gull	C	C	U	C
Glaucous Gull	R	R		X
Black-legged Kittiwake	Ue	Ue	Re	Ue
Sabine's Gull		Ue	Re	Re
Caspian Tern (B)	X	F	F	F
Royal Tern (B)	FL	U	UL	FL
Elegant Tern (B)	X	R	Ue	Fe
Common Tern		R	X	U
Arctic Tern		Ue	X	Ue
Forster's Tern (B)	F	C	F	C
Least Tern (+)		RL	RL	RL
Black Tern	X	X	X	X
Black Skimmer (B)	R	FL	FL	UL
Common Murre	C	C	C	C
Pigeon Guillemot	R	F	F	F
Marbled Murrelet	X	X	X	X
Xantus' Murrelet	R	X	X	R
Ancient Murrelet	Ue	Ue	X	Ue
Cassin's Auklet	F	F	U	F
Rhinoceros Auklet (b)	F	F	U	F
Tufted Puffin (?)		X	X	X
Horned Puffin	X	R		
Rock Dove (B)	C	C	C	C
Band-tailed Pigeon (B)	F	F	F	F
Spotted Dove	F	F	F	F
Mourning Dove (B)	C	C	C	C
Greater Roadrunner (B)	R	UL	R	UL
Barn Owl (B)	U	U	U	U

	W	Sp	Su	F
Flammulated Owl	U	FL	FL	FL
Western Screech-Owl (B)	F	F	F	F
Great Horned Owl (B)	F	F	F	F
Northern Pygmy-Owl (B)	F	F	F	F
Burrowing Owl (B)	R	RL	RL	R
Spotted Owl (B)	U	U	U	U
Long-eared Owl (b)	X	XL	XL	X
Short-eared Owl	Re	Re	RL	Re
Northern Saw-whet Owl (B)	U	U	UL	U
Common Poorwill (b)	X	UL	UL	R
Black Swift		R	RL	R
Vaux's Swift	X	F	UL	U
White-throated Swift (B)	U	U	U	U
Costa's Hummingbird (B)	R	FL	FL	U
Anna's Hummingbird (B)	C	C	C	C
Rufous Hummingbird		F	U	F
Allen's Hummingbird	F	C	C	U
Belted Kingfisher (B)	U	U	U	U
Lewis' Woodpecker	Re	Re		Re
Acorn Woodpecker (B)	F	F	F	F
Red-naped Sapsucker	R	X	X	R
Red-breasted Sapsucker (b)	U	U	XL	U
Nuttall's Woodpecker (B)	F	F	F	F
Downy Woodpecker (B)	F	F	F	F
Hairy Woodpecker (B)	F	F	F	F
Northern Flicker (B)	C	F	F	C
Olive-sided Flycatcher (B)		C	C	U
Western Wood-Pewee (B)		C	C	F
Willow Flycatcher (B)		R		R
Hammond's Flycatcher	X	X		X
Pacific-slope Flycatcher (B)	X	C	C	C
Black Phoebe (B)	F	F	F	F
Say's Phoebe (B)	F	U		F
Ash-throated Flycatcher (B)		F	F	U
Tropical Kingbird	X	X		R
Western Kingbird (B)		R	XL	R

	W	Sp	Su	F
Loggerhead Shrike (B)	U	U	RL	U
Cassin's Vireo (B)	X	F	F	F
Hutton's Vireo (B)	C	C	C	C
Warbling Vireo (B)	X	C	C	C
Steller's Jay (B)	C	C	C	C
Scrub Jay (B)	C	C	C	C
Clark's Nutcracker	UL	UL	UL	UL
American Crow (B)	F	F	FL	F
Common Raven (B)	F	F	F	F
Horned Lark (B)	U	UL	UL	U
Purple Martin (B)		R	RL	R
Tree Swallow (B)	U	F	F	F
Violet-green Swallow (B)	U	C	C	C
Northern Rough-winged Swallow (B)	X	F	F	F
Bank Swallow	X	FL	FL	U
Cliff Swallow		C	C	F
Barn Swallow (B)	X	C	C	C
Mountain Chickadee (B)	FL	U	U	FL
Oak Titmouse (B)	C	C	C	C
Bushtit (B)	C	C	C	C
Red-breasted Nuthatch (B)	Fe	Fe	U	Fe
White-breasted Nuthatch (B)	F	F	F	F
Pygmy Nuthatch (B)	C	C	C	C
Brown Creeper (B)	C	C	C	C
Rock Wren (B)	R	RL	RL	R
Bewick's Wren (B)	C	C	C	C
House Wren (B)	R	U	UL	U
Winter Wren (B)	F	F	F	F
Marsh Wren (B)	F	F	FL	F
American Dipper	RL	RL	RL	RL
Golden-crowned Kinglet	Fe	Fe	FL	Fe
Ruby-crowned Kinglet	C	F		C
Blue-gray Gnatcatcher (B)	R	U	UL	R
Western Bluebird (B)	U	U	U	U

Species	W	Sp	Su	F
Swainson's Thrush		C	C	C
Hermit Thrush	C	C	FL	C
American Robin (B)	C	C	C	C
Varied Thrush	Ce	Ce	XL	Ce
Wrentit (B)	C	C	C	C
Northern Mockingbird (B)	C	C	C	C
California Thrasher (B)	C	C	C	C
European Starling (B)	C	C	C	C
American Pipit	C	C		C
Cedar Waxwing	C	C	X	C
Phainopepla (B)		U	U	X
Tennessee Warbler	X	X	X	R
Orange-crowned Warbler (B)	U	C	C	C
Nashville Warbler	R	R		R
Northern Parula		X	R	X
Yellow Warbler (B)	X	F	F	C
Chestnut-sided Warbler		X	X	R
Magnolia Warbler		X	X	R
Yellow-rumped Warbler (B)	C	C	UL	C
Black-throated Gray Warbler (B)	R	F	F	F
Townsend's Warbler	C	C		C
Hermit Warbler	R	F	FL	F
Prairie Warbler	X	X		R
Palm Warbler	R	X		R
Blackpoll Warbler		X		R
Black-and-white Warbler	R	X	X	R
American Redstart	X	X	X	R
Northern Waterthrush	X		X	R
MacGillivray's Warbler	X	U	UL	U
Common Yellowthroat (B)	F	F	FL	F
Hooded Warbler		X	X	X
Wilson's Warbler	X	C	C	C
Yellow-breasted Chat (B)		R	U	U
Western Tanager (B)	X	F	UL	F
Rose-breasted Grosbeak	R	X	R	X
Black-headed Grosbeak (B)	X	C	C	C
Lazuli Bunting (B)		F	F	U
Indigo Bunting	X	X	X	X
California Towhee (B)	C	C	C	C
Rufous-crowned Sparrow (B)	RL	RL	RL	RL
Chipping Sparrow (B)	X	F	F	U
Clay-colored Sparrow	X	X		R
Lark Sparrow (B)	R	UL	UL	U
Savannah Sparrow (B)	C	F	F	C
Grasshopper Sparrow (B)	X	F	F	R
Fox Sparrow (B)	C	C		C
Song Sparrow (B)	C	C	C	C
Lincoln's Sparrow	F	F		F
Swamp Sparrow	R	X		R
White-throated Sparrow	R	R		R
Golden-crowned Sparrow	C	C		C
White-crowned Sparrow	C	C	C	C
Dark-eyed Junco (B)	C	C	C	C
Lapland Longspur	X	X		R
Bobolink		R	X	R
Red-winged Blackbird (B)	C	F	F	C
Tricolored Blackbird (B)	F	F	UL	F
Western Meadowlark (B)	C	F	F	C
Yellow-headed Blackbird	X	X	X	X
Brewer's Blackbird (B)	C	C	C	C
Brown-headed Cowbird (B)	U	C	C	F
Hooded Oriole (B)	X	F	F	U
Baltimore Oriole (B)	R	F	F	U
Purple Finch (B)	C	C	C	C
House Finch (B)	C	C	C	C
Red Crossbill	Ue	Ue	Re	Ue
Pine Siskin (B)	C	F	F	C
Lesser Goldfinch (B)	C	C	C	C
Lawrence's Goldfinch (b)	X	Re	Re	X
American Goldfinch (B)	C	C	C	C
Evening Grosbeak	Re	Re	X	Re
House Sparrow (B)	C	C	C	C

Index of Scientific Names

This index references only primary, illustrated species descriptions.

Index of Common Names

Boldface page numbers refer to primary, illustrated species descriptions.

About the Authors

When he's not out watching birds, frogs or snakes, Chris Fisher researches endangered species management and wildlife interpretation in the Department of Renewable Resources at the University of Alberta. The appeal of western wildlife and wilderness has led to many travels, including frequent visits with the birds of the Pacific coast. He is the author of *Birds of Seattle* and co-author of *Birds of Los Angeles* and *Birds of San Francisco*, and he still has more books up his sleeve. By sharing his enthusiasm and passion for wild things through lectures, photographs and articles, Chris strives to foster a greater appreciation for the value of our wilderness.

Herbert Clarke has studied birds all over the world, but he has a special fondness for the birds in his home state of California. He is the author of *An Introduction to Southern California Birds* and *An Introduction to Northern California Birds* and co-author of *Birds of the West*. Herbert has been an avid birder since childhood, and his writings and photographs have appeared in many prestigious books and magazines. When he is not on one of his frequent travels, he leads tours, gives illustrated lectures and instructs classes on birds. Herbert and Olga, his wife and constant field companion, live in Glendale, California.